The Real
OSCAR
WILDE

'The truth is rarely pure & never simple'
Oscar Wilde

For Ophelia, my small shadow

For Matthew Pateman, Lee Murray, Rob Jeffrey
& Rob Lane - Thank you for 2024

The Real

OSCAR WILDE

Laura Brennan

WHITE OWL

AN IMPRINT OF PEN & SWORD BOOKS LTD
YORKSHIRE - PHILADELPHIA

First published in Great Britain in 2025 by
PEN AND SWORD WHITE OWL
An imprint of
Pen & Sword Books Ltd
Yorkshire – Philadelphia

ISBN 978 1 39905 898 8

Typeset in Times New Roman 11.5/15.5 by
SJmagic DESIGN SERVICES, India.
Printed and bound in the UK by CPI Group (UK) Ltd, Croydon, CR0 4YY.

The Publisher's authorised representative in the EU for product safety is
Authorised Rep Compliance Ltd., Ground Floor, 71 Lower Baggot Street,
Dublin D02 P593, Ireland.
www.arccompliance.com

For a complete list of Pen & Sword titles please contact

PEN & SWORD BOOKS LIMITED
George House, Units 12 & 13, Beevor Street, Off Pontefract Road,
Barnsley, South Yorkshire, S71 1HN, England
E-mail: enquiries@pen-and-sword.co.uk
Website: www.pen-and-sword.co.uk

or

PEN AND SWORD BOOKS
1950 Lawrence Rd, Havertown, PA 19083, USA
E-mail: uspen-and-sword@casematepublishers.com
Website: www.penandswordbooks.com

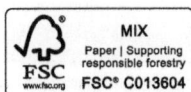

MIX
Paper | Supporting
responsible forestry
FSC® C013604

CONTENTS

PUBLISHED WORKS TIMELINE

Genre	Year	Title
Poetry	1878	*Ravenna*
Poetry	1880s	*Requiescat*
Play	1880	*Vera/The Nihilists*
Poetry	1881	First Collection of Poems
Play	1883	*The Duchess of Padua*
Essay	1885	'The Philosophy of Dress'
Short Fiction	1888	*The Happy Prince & Other Stories*
Essay	1889	'The Decay of Lying'
Essay	1889	'Pen, Pencil and Poison'
Novel	1890	*The Picture of Dorian Gray*
Essay	1891	'The Soul of Man under Socialism'
Essay	1891	'Intentions' (Collection of Essays)
Short Fiction	1891	*A House of Pomegranates*
Short Fiction	1891	*Lord Arthur Savile's Crimes and Other Stories*
Play	1892	*Lady Windermere's Fan*
Play	1893	*A Woman of No Importance*
Play	1893	*Salomé* (In France)
Essay	1894	'Phrases and Philosophies for the Use of the Young'

Genre	Year	Title
Essay	1894	'A few maxims for the instruction of the over-Educated'
Poetry	1894	*The Sphinx*
Poetry	1894	*Poems in Prose*
Play	1895	*An Ideal Husband*
Play	1895	*The Importance of Being Earnest*
Poetry	1898	*The Ballad of Reading Gaol*

Posthumous Publications

De Profundis – 1905 – An edited version
1913 – A Suppressed Version
1962 – Full Version

The Rise of Historical Criticism – 1905 & 1908

The first collection edition of fourteen Volumes in 1908 – this collection of work contained previously unpublished works

The second collection edition twelve volumes published 1909–11 included previously unpublished works.

The Women of Homer (1876) published in 2008

ACKNOWLEDGEMENTS

It is fair to say that as much as writing a book can be a solitary activity it cannot be completed (or so I have found) without the support, encouragement and advice from others.

First, I would like to take this opportunity to thank Jonathan Wright for suggesting the title and being (as aways) supportive, and the ever efficient Laura Hirst. This thanks, of course, extends to all the staff at White Owl Books and Pen & Sword; without your faith in me, I could not have made a childhood dream come true four times now.

To my editor Karyn Burnham thank you. I would like to take this opportunity to apologise for some of those oddly worded sentences that you had to unravel to make sense. The skill of being able to fine tune an author's work, but keep the essence of the author's style is something I will never stop being grateful for.

To the staff at the British Library, thank you for your patience and help tracking down books. My uncles Paul Brennan and Peter Bradley, again thank you for your encouragement and faith in me, as well as the lunches and chocolate – vital essentials for finishing a book. Thanks also needs to be given to Dan Wilson for his interest and optimism in this book, I hope I have done Oscar proud. My thanks also goes to Sean Lang for his encouragement and support. To Ruth Sullivan, Julia Hopkins and Kerry Park, thank you for being the best friends a girl can have and for your support and friendship. Many thanks also go to Haley Foster for her enthusiasm and history memes. To Emma and Nachiket Dave, thank you for your kindness and friendship.

Honourable mention should go to the subject of the book himself, Oscar Fingal O'Flahertie Wills Wilde. Since secondary school I have – sometimes without realising it – quoted Wilde; I have watched his plays and the subsequent films of those plays, and the films about his life. Several times as an adult I have visited Oscar's grave in Paris's famous Père Lachaise cemetery, as well visit the hotel in which he died. Only during the research for this book did I realise that Mr Oscar Wilde had been part of my life since I was 15 years old. It will remain a life-long association.

Lastly, a big thank you goes out to anyone who has bought, read, borrowed, reviewed and recommended any of my books – including this one. I could not do this without an audience curious to know what I have to say about historical figures. I am always touched by your kind words and support.

Laura Brennan
February 2025

INTRODUCTION

Initially when I was approached to write this biography I was slightly concerned that a straight female should be tackling such a gay icon. It wasn't until I started my research that I realised there was far more to Mr Oscar Fingal O'Flahertie Wills Wilde than someone who was exposed as gay later in life, during a period when homosexuality was illegal. So while that is a very important aspect of his story, this book also explores the other, lesser well-known parts of his life.

From the beginning, Oscar's childhood was extraordinary. His parents were over achievers in their own right; academically, he would shine and win scholarships for those subjects at which he excelled – Greek language and history. Thanks to his mother, Lady Wilde, Oscar had the opportunity to mix with the extraordinary people of literature and culture in Dublin. Lady Wilde often held salon style gatherings, inviting artists, writers and academics into the family home. This was a tradition Wilde himself continued when he was at Oxford University.

Oscar the public speaker and poet is less known today, but it was during these early years as he was starting to make a name for himself, that he was able to cultivate and create the persona of Oscar Wilde – the colourful and witty man we think of today. The speaking tour of the United States of America that he undertook in 1882 aged 28, brought the concepts of the Aesthetic Movement across the Atlantic. These aspects of himself, the poet, the aesthete, the wit and the dandy, would in turn appear in various different ways throughout his works. It was through his aestheticism that Oscar was able to influence and support causes such as the Arts and Crafts Movement, and even women's dress reform.

Oscar Wilde had genuine affection and love for his wife Constance, who would support him and remain on good terms with him for the rest of her life. This would not have been easy for her, personally or socially, after his very public outing and conviction, especially during the conservative Victorian period. The pair never divorced. She even visited him twice in prison personally tell him his mother had died because she wanted the news to be broken to him in a kind and gentle manner. Although their correspondence was not always amicable in later years, there was a bond and respect between them. Oscar also owned the fact that he had done wrong by both Constance and their two boys – something that takes great courage and much contemplation. When Constance died in 1898, Wilde was genuinely grief-stricken by the news. Theirs was a mutual, respectful love that changed over time, but their friendship and bond over their children was strong until the end.

Oscar Wilde the father was another facet of this great man that I found both moving – and important in understanding the real Oscar Wilde. His legacy would live on through his son Vyvyan, who, like his father, had a fascination with the Catholic Church and converted to the faith, was a writer and – despite his disrupted childhood – was a man of great empathy and compassion who would never resent or hate his father, even after his mother's family became his guardian following her death in 1898.

I have tried to remain consistent throughout the book; for example, when Oscar's son Vyvyan changed the spelling of his first name to the more conventional Vivian, I decided to kept the original spelling, as he did revert to the original spelling himself a few years later. Wilde refers to Robert Ross both as Bobbie and Robbie in the letters he writes to him. As Ross is most widely known today as Robbie, I used this when writing about him, and only using 'Bobbie' in direct quotations. The majority of the time I refer to Lord Alfred Douglas by his moniker 'Bosie', again this is for consistency and also because it is the name he is best known by. Any money conversions mentioned have been calculated by the National Archives historic money converter.

Lastly, this is a biography that seeks to showcase the *real* Oscar Wilde. Homosexuality was just one of many facets of the man, and he deserves to be remembered for more than the scandal that changed his life in 1895.

Prior to starting this project I was familiar with the better-known works by Wilde, indeed I did not realise how much I quoted Oscar in every day speech. I knew some of his most famous quotes, but did not know that they were accredited to him. Years ago, prior to the Plexiglass being erected around his tomb in Père Lachaise cemetery in Paris, I, like many before me, had made the pilgrimage to visit his grand tomb and kissed the grave with my trademark red lipstick. Little did I know that about fifteen years later I would be writing this book about him. When I went back to visit him on a beautiful blue-skied May morning in 2023, a part of me felt that the Oscar I have discovered through my research would have been saddened by the glass protecting his grave monument from his readers and admirers. In his later life, while in exile, Oscar wrote to Robbie Ross in a letter, 'I need love and to be loved', and through his legacy of work, his courage in accepting who he was, Oscar Wilde has continued to be loved and remains relevant, and still touches people emotionally well into the twenty-first century.

THE SEEDS OF GENIUS

'Relations are simply a tedious pack of people who
haven't got the remotest knowledge of how to live, nor
smallest instinct when to die.'

The Importance of Being Earnest

To some degree, our parents help shape us into the people we become; whether by us following their example, or deliberately choosing to live in a way opposite to the experiences of our formative years. There are, of course, inherited characteristics – both physical and behavioural, some of which we cannot change. All these things come together to create the uniqueness of each of us. In the case of Oscar Fingal O'Flahertie Wills Wilde, it is clear that he developed, and inherited, many of the characteristics we associate with him today from both his mother and his father. That is why it is important to explore both of his parents before delving deeper into Oscar himself.

The paternal side of Oscar Wilde's family arrived in Ireland during the late 1680s, in the aftermath of the Glorious Revolution, which saw James II & VII, lose his thrones to his son-in-law and nephew, William III of Orange and his own daughter, Mary. In an attempt to regain his thrones in England, Scotland and Wales, James managed to bring the Williamite War to Ireland. Among the battles fought was the infamous Battle of the Boyne, in July 1690. Colonel de Wilde, was a Dutch solider who came over with William of Orange and decided to remain in Ireland after the war, making it his new home. Over the years the 'de' was dropped but the Protestant faith of the 'de Wildes' remained. This explains why, in the 1850s, the Wilde family were Protestant in a predominately Catholic Dublin. That said, at that time, Ireland was still united as one country and under British rule, so the men sent to rule Ireland were Protestant administrators and prominent within Victorian Dublin society.

The Wildes had worked hard and prospered, enabling later generations to flourish and thrive in Ireland. Oscar's great-grandfather, Ralph Wilde, was a farmer and land agent in County Roscommon towards the north-west of the country. Ralph Wilde was prosperous and successful enough to be able to educate his eldest son in Dublin for a career in the church, and have his middle son Thomas (Oscar's grandfather) train as a doctor across the Irish sea in England. Ralph Wilde's third son, William, was financed to relocate to the Caribbean in order to make his fortune in the Jamaican sugar plantations.

Following his medical training, Dr Thomas Wilde returned to County Roscommon, where he quickly established a thriving medical practice. He would marry Amelia Flynne and they would go on and have five surviving children; two daughters and three sons, one of which was Oscar's father, William Robert Wilde.

William Robert followed in his father's footsteps and trained to become a medical doctor. He choose to specialise in surgery of the ear, nose, throat, neck and eye. Dr Wilde moved east, to the city of Dublin, where he settled down and married Oscar's equally fascinating mother, Jane Francesca Agnes Elgee in the winter of 1851.

Like William, Jane was a member of the Church of Ireland, the Irish Protestant part of the Anglican communion, rather than be part of the predominately Roman Catholic communion. This Anglican leaning passed through several previous generations when her great-grandfather, Charles Elgee, immigrated to Ireland from the North East of England. He and his brother were builders, one specialising in carpentry, the other bricklaying, and they moved to take advantage of the building boom in the early eighteenth century. It was a good move because the family flourished and remained upon Irish shores.

The next generation of the Elgee family, one John Elgee, would go to Trinity College, Dublin, before entering the Church of Ireland. He married a Jane Waddyin in late 1782 and the following year, 1783, Lady Wilde's father, Charles Elgee, was born. He would be the first of seven children.

Charles Elgee, Oscar's maternal grandfather, would become a solicitor in Dublin. In 1809, he married Lady Wilde's mother, Sarah Kingsbury. The Kingsburys were also well established within Dublin society, with both medical doctors and respectable men of the church within the family. However, this did not stop the formative years of their married life from being somewhat turbulent. The couple would suffer from money troubles, causing them to frequently change address.

Jane Elgee, later Lady Wilde, was the last child of the couple's marriage. Jane was rather ambiguous about her official age and date of birth. This ambiguity has caused historians and biographers much confusion and this frustrating and vain habit would later be adopted by Oscar. It is most commonly agreed that her date of birth was 27 December 1821. This date had been found on an application form for the Royal Literary Fund, which incidentally was successful, and they granted her the sum of £100.

Eighteen months after Jane's birth, her parents' turbulent marriage came to an end with the death of her father, Charles. The exact circumstance of his death are not known and no explanation was given in the obituary in the *Freeman's Journal*, published on 4 February 1825. The article merely mentioned that Charles had died on 13 August 1824 while out in Bangalore, India. Given the period, we can make an educated guesses that Charles may have found a job with the East India Company. India was the jewel in the British Empire's large crown. As to the cause of his death, he may have succumbed to malaria, like many other English and Irishmen who went to seek their fortunes in India, although we will never know for sure.

Lady Wilde's childhood with her widowed mother Sarah Elgee would not have been a traditional Victorian upbringing and might perhaps explain some of Lady Wilde's more liberal and eccentric behaviours and views in later life. As a result of her disruptive childhood, she had received what can only be described as a patchy education, which is surprising given her literary achievements later in life. She was always an avid reader and was able to teach herself several European languages. She would speak of this period of her life in a magazine article published in *Hearth & Home* in June 1896: 'I was very fond of study and books. My favourite study was languages. I succeeded in mastering ten of the European languages. Till my eighteenth year I never wrote anything. All my time was given to study.'

Lady Jane's eccentric and rebellious streak was recognised by her family and they nicknamed her 'the rebel'. These childhood experiences with her widowed mother certainly would have made her more resilient, independent and strong-willed in nature than the average nineteenth-century young woman of her class.

As an adult, one of Lady Wilde's eccentric claims was that her maiden name, Elgee, was an anglicised and bastardised form of the Italian surname Algiati, which was of course is the surname of Italy's most famous thirteenth century poet, Dante. This is something of a tall tale, with great entertainment value – though no doubt, Lady Wilde hoped this would help her own reputation as a writer, particularly of poetry. But she need not have worried; she, like her younger son Oscar, was a critically acclaimed success in this genre of literature, as well as gaining wide recognition through her many passionate political writings.

Aware that as a female writer she would be taken less seriously than her male counterparts, Jane would adopt a nom de plume that echoed her tall tales of Italian ancestry. The pen name she choose was 'Speranza', meaning Hope. She also had a personal motto: *Fidanza, Speranza, Costanza*, meaning Faith, Hope and Consistency.

Unlike many of her peers, Jane Elgee was still unmarried in her late twenties. This was to change in September 1849, when she wrote a particularly favourable review of Dr William Wilde's book *The Beauties of the Boyne and its Tributary the Blackwater*, for the journal *The Nation*. Within the book itself, William had quoted one of Jane's poems while describing the banks of the River Boyne. It is likely that both William and Jane would have met prior to her positive review of his book, as both moved in similar circles with a similar political, literary and social standing. Romance blossomed between the pair and they married in St Peter's church, Dublin, on 12 November 1851, with the service conducted by Wilde's brother, Rev. John M. Wilde. Both of these highly intelligent and talented individuals had met their equal.

The Wildes were blessed with two sons and a daughter. Their eldest, William (Wille) Charles Kingsbury, was born on the 26 September 1852. Two years later, on 16 October 1854, Oscar arrived, and finally Isola Francesca Emily was born on 2 April 1857. These were not Sir William's only recognised children, however. He also had two daughters (Emily and Mary), and a son (Henry Wilson) by other women prior to marrying Lady Wilde. Henry Wilson would follow in his father's footsteps and train to be a doctor within the same fields. Father and son worked together in Wilde's Dublin practice.

Emily and Mary were also acknowledged, and took William's surname as their own. They lived with Sir William's brother, Rev. Ralph Wilde, in County Monaghan. One cold and snowy November evening in 1871, both sisters attended a local dance. While dancing near a fire, Emily's dress caught fire. When Mary saw what had happened she went to her sister's aid and in her efforts to try and help Emily, her own dress also caught fire. The sisters were brought outside to the snow in an attempt to help their burns but both had suffered injuries too severe to be able to survive. This saddened Sir William in the later years of his life.

Two years after his marriage, Dr Wilde would be one of the founders of an ophthalmic hospital called St Mark's in central Dublin. His good work within his specialist areas would catch the attention of Queen Victoria, who would go on and create a post especially for him, the Surgeon Oculist in Ordinary to the Queen. This was an honorary position, and did not require the family to move to England. Queen Victoria would further recognise Dr Wilde by knighting him in 1864. His knighthood was for his work in collecting data for the Irish census, rather than for his medical career and work.

Wilde enjoyed his early career success and even royal recognition within Dublin, he would, like his second son Oscar, end his professional success under a cloud of sexual scandal. On 12 December 1864, a libel trial opened at Dublin's court of common pleas that saw Sir William was accused of sexually assaulting one of his female patients. The woman in question was Mary Josephine Travers. She accused Wilde of taking advantage of her under the administration of a small amount of chloroform (still being used as an anaesthetic during this period). The chloroform meant that she was unable to resist his inappropriate and non-consensual advances.

Sir William, along with his wife, Lady Wilde, sued his accuser Mary Travers for libel. Inevitably, as in cases like this during the nineteenth century, the female victims name and reputation was called into question, and she was cross-examined in the most damning of ways. Given the period in which she lived, it was extremely brave of her to have even accused an ennobled man of such a crime, many other women would have said nothing. Not surprisingly, due to the status and minor celebrity of the man accused, the case caused a scandalous sensation at the time in Dublin.

Although Mary Travers technically won her case against Wilde, she was made aware of what the court felt through the sum of money awarded to her as compensation. Her reputation and her ordeal were only worth the lowly sum of just one farthing. The real justice in this situation was that Wilde's reputation, both professionally and personally, never fully recovered from the scandal of his trial. This was due in part because he refused to take the stand, feeling it was both insulting and demeaning. This refusal to defend his name and reputation caused many to assume that the accusations were true.

Mary Travers' boldness and refusal to be quiet about the whole episode was yet more evident when she took to posting unpleasant letters through the letterboxes of the fashionable homes of Dublin's Merrion Square. Unsavoury articles about Dr Wilde appeared in the *Dublin Weekly Advertiser*, including disclosing that he had three illegitimate children. Travers was most likely the source of that information. Finally, when Lady Wilde went to Bray – a coastal town 20km from Dublin – to avoid this harassment, Travers not only followed her, but she persuaded local newspaper lads to hold placards outside where she was staying, offering for sale scandal pamphlets about the Wildes. While staying in Bray and suffering this new humiliation from Mary Travers, Lady Wilde decided to write to the young woman's father about her behaviour and in the letter she described Mary's behaviour as a disgrace.

For the last years of his life, Sir William devoted his time building a house near Lough Corrib, in County Galway, where he would later take up residence, choosing to shy away from Dublin society. It was here that he was able to pursue his other scholarly passions within the fields of Natural History and ethnology.

Throughout his adulthood, Sir William published no less than twenty books on a variety of subjects. One of his better-known volumes is the book reviewed by Jane, *The Beauties of the Boyne and the Blackwater*, but he also wrote and published several highly regarded textbooks in his specialised medical fields of ear, nose, throat, neck and eye health, many of which were used well into the twentieth century.

Sir William Wilde died on 19 April 1876 at the age of 61. Despite the previous scandal that had cause Dr Wilde shy away from Dublin society, he was still so well thought of that the Lord Mayor of Dublin, Lord Chancellor of Ireland, Lord Chief Justice, the president of the Royal Irish academy and an array of fellows form Trinity College Dublin all attended his funeral. He was laid to rest at the family vault in Mount Jerome Cemetery, Dublin.

Lady Wilde would go on to live a further twenty years after her husband death. She relocated to London with both her sons after Oscar graduated from Oxford university in 1878, where she remained until her death. Throughout her widowhood, particularly throughout her time in London, Lady Wilde struggled for money, often asking her sons for financial support. While she was in her final illness – a case of nasty Bronchitis – she requested to visit her Oscar in prison, but her request was refused by the authorities. On the night that she died, aged 75, on 3 February 1896, Oscar vividly dreamed about his mother even though he had no knowledge of his mother's illness. Her funeral took place two days later on 5 February at Kensal Green Cemetery, London, where she was buried anonymously without even a headstone to mark her grave. In 1996 a plaque was added to her husband's grave in Mount Jerome Cemetery, Dublin. Three years later in 1999, the Oscar Wilde Society erected a Celtic cross dedicated to Lady Wilde in Kensal Green Cemetery. It was a sad end for an extraordinary woman

Considering the historical context into which the Wilde children were born helps create an insight into some of Oscar's behaviours, views and politics. It also highlights how modern and enlightened Oscar was, given that he was living in a Victorian society with very distinct, traditional and moral social expectations.

Oscar was born into a Dublin that was still part of a united Ireland, as well as part of the British Empire. The reigning monarch was Queen Victoria, and she had been on the throne for nearly two decades. The division of Ireland as we understand it today, with two different countries upon one isle, the Republic of Ireland and Northern Ireland did not happen until twenty-one years after his death. Although predominantly a Catholic country, the Wilde family were typical of their social class and of the Anglo-Irish community and society within Dublin; they were Anglican Protestants rather than Catholics, well educated, outward-looking and affluent. Outside of Dublin, the vast majority of Protestants within Ireland were further north, in what is Northern Ireland today.

It is therefore little wonder that, given his parents and his upbringing, Oscar Wilde, was able to bloom and grow into such an intellectual and literary genius. The moral, political and social behaviours of his parents also influenced his beliefs and how he chose to live his life. Had he had a far more traditional Victorian upbringing, I suspect we would never have had the literary and dramatical works he left to us.

CHILDHOOD AND EARLY EDUCATION

'All women become like their mothers. That is their tragedy.
No man does, and that is his.'
The Importance of Being Earnest

Dublin in the autumn can mainly be described as grey and wet, but on 16 October 1854, Dr Wilde and Lady Jane Wilde welcomed their second son into the world. The baby boy's name was Oscar Fingal O'Flahertie Wills Wilde, a grand name for such a small baby; but a name that he would grow into, and a name that would become known not only in his native country of Ireland, but in Britian, Europe, across the Atlantic in North America and even Australia during his lifetime.

Oscar Wilde would become known for his persona, politics, poetry, novels, short stories and plays, as well as become the leading light of the Aesthetic movement and become one of the first public figures to start breaking down social, political and legal thinking in regards towards homosexuality. And for doing so he would pay a heavy price personally, socially and professionally, simply for loving a man.

Oscar had an elder brother William (Willie), born just shy of two years before on the 26 September 1852. The two brothers were be joined by a sister, Isola, in the spring of 1857. Isola, however, had a tragically short life; she died on the 23 February 1867 at the age of just 10. Isola had contracted a fever which subsequently developed into an effusion on the brain – this in layman's terms means she developed fluid in the brain which then became infected. Although we cannot know for certain, one possible cause may have been meningitis. Her death particularly affected Oscar, with whom she had been closest.

Both Willie and Oscar were born in the Wildes' first family home located on Westland Row, Dublin. Within a year of Oscar being born, however, the family moved several streets away to a bigger house and a better neighbourhood in Dublin. Number 1 Merrion Square was the largest home on the road and it gave the family room to grow, as well as giving Dr Wilde a place to operate his practice from. The family home had one entrance, and there was a separate entrance for his patients.

Merrion Square would famously host 'Speranza's' (Jane's nom de plume) literary salons and welcome the greats of the arts world from Dublin and beyond. It would also be home to Oscar during his freshman year at Trinity College Dublin, conveniently located within walking distance of the Wildes' home. It would remain the family home until Oscar later graduated from Oxford, and Lady Wilde decided to follow her sons to London rather than stay in Dublin alone.

Oscar was particularly close to his mother and this relationship remained close throughout his life adult years. The pair held many views in common as well as having a shared love of literature and poetry. Speranza encouraged and fed the young Oscar's love of the arts and she even allowed both Willie and Oscar to join the literary salons she held in their home on Merrion Square. While at these Salons both Willie and Oscar were only allow to speak if spoken to, but they would have met and listened to many the great and good Irish and English literary greats of the day. This love of literature was further encouraged by Lady Wilde when she read to her children, starting from a very young age. She exposed them to the works of Tennyson and Poe, as well as sharing her own poetry with the boys. Oscar was particularly fond of one of his mother's poems about the Sheares Brothers.

The poem in question is in the style of a ballad, one of Speranza's favourite forms of poetry and was entitled The Brothers and tells the story of two Irish brothers, Henry and John Sheares, who were executed for their role in the 1798 Irish Rebellion, an insurrection of Irish nationals against British rule of Ireland. Wilde praised his mother's politics in public several times, most notably in the US on St Patrick's day 1882, in a speech made at St Paul, Minnesota.

Jane Wilde also took her children on holidays in the summer to various idyllic parts of Ireland including Bray in County Wicklow and across the country to Connemara. It was in Connemara that Oscar's father, Dr Wilde built a holiday home facing the Atlantic coastline. The Wilde boys' childhood was, in many ways conventional for middle-class Anglo-Irish family.

Dr Wilde certainly loved all his children, both legitimate and illegitimate, and unlike many men during the Victorian period, Dr Wilde did not hide his illegitimate children from his wife or his other children. He was a busy and established professional man, who had a busy medical practice, established a hospital in Dublin as well as having many outside interests, including writing books about Irish history and medical text books. He also played a major role in collecting data for the Irish census.

Oscar, like his father, seems to have not seen infidelity as particularly wrong. When Oscar was just 10 years old, his father faced accusations of sexually assaulting one of his patients, Mary Josephine Travers, while she was under the influence of chloroform. The subsequent accusations led to a court hearing. Using the courts to sue for libel is something Oscar would also do in 1895. These experiences in court were detrimental to the professional and social lives of both father and son. It is sad that Oscar had not learnt from his father's errors.

The year prior to his sister's sudden and unexpected death, an 11-year-old Oscar had joined Willie at Portora Royal School, a boarding school based near Enniskillen (now part of Northern Ireland). The school dated back to the reign of the Stuarts in the early seventeenth century and was considered one of the leading schools within Ireland during the mid-nineteenth century when Oscar and Willie attended.

The fees paid by the Wildes' to send their boys to the school were fairly reasonable at £17.10s an academic term. The amount was lowered by the fact that their father was a doctor and the boys were expected to go on and study at Trinity College Dublin. Oscar's time at Portora Royal included mandatory attendance of chapel as part of the school day, and this soured his feelings towards religion – in particular towards the Protestant Church of Ireland.

During his first few years at Portora Royal, Oscar was academically outshone by his elder brother's achievements in the classroom. Although he preferred books to sport, and he particularly disliked football and cricket, Oscar did enjoy the athletic activities offered to students, such as running. Eventually, he found a subject in which he would flourish academically. In his final year at the school, the young Oscar would go on to win academic medals in Greek Testament (the study of the biblical texts in the original Greek), and the study of the Classics. These achievements enabled Oscar to win a scholarship to Trinity College Dublin and join Willie, who was already studying there.

On 10 October 1871, Oscar sat the matriculation exams to study at Trinity, Dublin. His time at Portora Royal had prepared him well as he excelled in Greek, Latin and history – although not so much in mathematics. If we needed proof that arithmetic was not Wilde's strongest skill, we need only look at his finances later in life. As Oscar's fresher year started, he opted to remain living at Merrion Square, given its close proximity to the university campus. This arrangement did not last more than an academic year, and for his second and third years he moved to campus to enjoy the freedoms of student life.

As a student of Classics, Wilde's attendance come at the most advantageous time as the department had just had a refresh of the teaching staff. The two new staff that would revamp the reputation of the Classics department for academic excellence, and both would play important roles within Wilde's time at Trinity as an undergraduate. Their enthusiasm for their subjects was infectious to an Oscar who was eager to learn. These two new members of staff were Robert Tyrrell and Reverend John Mahaffy. Both new Dons had been Trinity graduates, and yet both men had very different styles of teaching. Despite their differences, Wilde found that he was academically drawn to both men.

Tyrrell was only 27 when he joined the Classics department. His official title was Professor of Latin, however his true passion was Greek literature and so it's easy to see why Wilde favoured Tyrrell. His lectures often strayed from the set theme and he indulged in teaching his real passion of Greek literature. His youth also made him more approachable to the students than many of their other professors.

Reverend John Mahaffy was five years older than Tyrrell, although he too was relatively young to have been elevated to the position of professor at 32 years old. Unlike Tyrrell, he was far less approachable, and he had the speech impediment known as rhotacism – this is the inability to pronounce the letter R correctly. Both Oscar and his elder brother Willie had known Mahaffy prior to him teaching at Trinity as he had been a regular attendee at their mother's salons in Merrion Square.

Whereas Tyrrell was interested in the language of ancient Greece and Latin, Mahaffy's interest was focused on the life and society of these ancient civilisations, with a particular interest in the Greeks and Romans. He, like many nineteenth-century academics within their field, felt that the modern world could learn much from these advanced societies that had thrived thousands of years earlier – although there would be exceptions to what Victorian society should accept and bring back. Unfortunately, Mahaffy did not agree with the sexual liberation of these ancient societies, especially the Greeks' openly homosexual relations and their acceptance of relationships between older and younger men.

One of the most important skills that Wilde learnt from his years at Trinity was the skill of great conversation and how to do it well. It is a important skill to be able to balance all the elements required of a good conversation and hold an audience's attention. Generally, the discussion should be a balance of wit, self-deprecation and flattery, all while displaying knowledge of the subject in question as well as actively listening to the other person or persons. This is a skill that is particularly cherished by the Irish. Of course, Wilde had be lucky enough to be exposed to some of the greatest talkers and conversationalists in Ireland and the UK at his mother's salons from a very early age.

His time at Trinity allowed Oscar to develop his own unique conversational style and create the persona of Oscar Wilde that we think of today. This skill would also help Wilde with his writing, particularly in his novel *The Picture of Dorian Gray,* and with the characters' dialogues in his plays. These dialogues are vital in the telling of the stories and successfully communicating with, and holding the attention of, an audience.

On the whole, Oscar was a conscientious student; his application to hard work and his studies would have been greatly helped by the fact that he was not particularly fond of his fellow classmates. When he was not following his set curriculum Wilde enjoyed discovering the great writers of the English language. These included reading and discovering the works of the American poet and essayist Walt Whitman, and American Gothic writer, poet and novelist, Edgar Allan Poe. However, there was one author that truly captured Wilde's attention at this time, and would become an influence throughout his life and career – the English poet, playwright and novelist, Algernon Swinburne,

Swinburne's work included pieces based on Greek myth and legends as well as Greek poet Sappho, so he would have appealed to Oscar. Swinburne also had links to the Pre-Raphaelite Brotherhood, including Dante Gabrielle Rossetti. The Pre-Raphaelite were the forerunners of the Aesthetic Movement, in which Wilde would become a leading figure. In short, the persona Oscar Wilde would become developed during his time as an undergraduate at Trinity College Dublin.

At the end of his first year at Trinity, Oscar had come top of his year within the Classics department. He decided to try for a foundation scholarship for his second year and he would be one of ten that were lucky to be granted this funding by college itself. In order to be awarded this scholarship, Oscar had to sit papers in Latin, Greek translation and English composition. Wilde managed to come first in both the English composition and Greek translation papers. This award would pay for his academic fees for the following year, and entitled him to rooms on campus with an additional £20 for his own expenses (£20 in the 1870s is roughly equivalent to £1,250 today, according to the National Archives currency converter online).

His second year at Trinity also ended in academic triumph when he would went on to win the Berkley Gold Medal for Greek. This would also be his last year at the Dublin university. Rev. Mahaffy suggested that Oscar continue his student career at Oxford. This move signified the end of his permanent residence in his native homeland of Ireland. During the summer of 1874, Lady Wilde, Willie and Oscar crossed the Irish Sea and Oscar went to Oxford to sit the scholarship exams. Of course he won the awarded funds and became a student of Magdalen College Oxford.

For most of the rest of that summer, the three Wildes enjoyed their time in London, celebrating Oscar's scholarship. They would cross the Chanel to visit Switzerland and Paris before finally returning to Dublin. Once back in Dublin, and prior to starting his studies at Oxford, Oscar had the opportunity to work on the manuscript of Rev. Mahaffy's new book on Greece, *Social Life in Greece from Homer to Menander*. Wilde's contribution was gratefully received by the author, and was duly credited in the work's acknowledgements: 'Mr Wilde of Magdalen College Oxford … for having made improvements and corrections all throughout the book.' (Mahaffy, Rev. J, *Social life in Greece from Homer to Menander*)

One of the sections that Oscar worked on dealt with the topic of homosexual relationships within ancient Greek society. Having studied Greek and Greek literature since his schooldays, this was by no means Oscar's introduction to the subject of homosexuality within Greece. He was, after all, a former boarding-school boy – though later in life Wilde stated that as boys they were more interested in sport than sex while at school.

Sadly, the friendship between Mahaffy and Wilde would not withstand the more scandalous aspects of Oscar's life. Twenty years later, when Oscar found himself facing charges of gross indecency, Mahaffy was horrified at the accusations, particularly that the men in question were much younger than Wilde – to him, the most distasteful part of the scandal – ironic given his specialism in Greek culture.

OSCAR THE OXFORD YEARS, 1874–8

'Education is an admirable thing, but
remember from time to time
that nothing that is worth knowing can be taught.'

Oscar Wilde

Wilde's time at Oxford was certainly not a poverty-stricken experience. His scholarship granted him an allowance of £95 per year, that comes to roughly £6,000 – no small sum for a student in the nineteenth century (National Archives currency converter). This grant was also supplemented by his over-indulgent parents. This extra financial support from his parents lasted until the death of his father, in 1876. His healthy financial situation meant that he was able to indulge in far better living quarters than many of his peers.

The romantic poet in Wilde fell in love with the university city of Oxford with all its charm, beauty and history, both within the town and the surrounding countryside. Compared to Dublin's Trinity College, he found both Magdalen college and his fellow students far more to his tastes.

Although he had completed two years' study at Trinity, Wilde had not completed a full degree course and so he was required to undertake the matriculation examinations the day after his twentieth birthday, 17 October 1874. Although older than many of his peers, his youthful, clean shaven face, made him appear much younger. It was his towering six foot plus height and broad-shouldered stature that distinguished him from his shorter undergraduate peers.

Magdalen suited Wilde's laid-back, gentle intelligence and unlike his time at Trinity, he was able to build a social circle of like-minded intelligent youths. Academically he felt under stretched by the work set because, compared to his peers, he had already two years of university learning under his belt. The bonus to this was that he was able to show off his skills in Greek, and would also play truant to lectures in pursuit of finding more challenging ideas to discuss. One such attraction outside of his curriculum was writer, critic and philosopher, John Ruskin.

Born in 1819, John Ruskin would become one of the Victorian era's most accomplished men. By the time that he had been made the first Slade Professor of Fine Arts at the University of Oxford in 1869, Ruskin had already had a dazzling carer as art critic and historian, philosopher and writer. He had been supported the work of J.M.W. Turner and the Pre-Raphaelite Brotherhood and the Arts and Craft Movement. While at Oxford he established the Ruskin School of Drawing and Fine Art. He was popular both with the university students as well as the general public and would often get the same lecture twice – once for his students and again, for the general public. It is easy to see why Oscar was interested in attending his lectures and cultivating a friendship with Ruskin. Indeed, Lady Wilde had been a fan of Ruskin, and Wilde already had a deep respect for his works and reputation by the time he got to Oxford. But most importantly of all, we can give Ruskin some credit for expanding Oscar's knowledge of the Renaissance Art in Florence; he introduced Wilde to such artists as Giotto, Fra Angelico and Botticelli.

It was not just the subjects that Wilde studied, he was enchanted by Ruskin's use of words, both spoken and written. Indeed, Oscar thought his new idolised luminary was the 'Plato of England', and coming from a Classicist there was no greater compliment or comparison he could make. These extra-curricular activities, however, would come to haunt Wilde when he failed to pass the 'responses exam' at the end of his first term. He was made to retake the exam, which he thankfully passed and saved his position at the university.

After completing his first year at Oxford, Wilde wanted to see the subjects of Ruskin's talks for himself and he travelled to Italy during the summer of 1874. Everything about Italy pleased him, the country bewitched him. His travels were not made alone, as he met with his former Trinity Professor, Rev. John Mahaffy, who was travelling with another of his students. The threesome travelled on a mini Grand Tour of Italy, taking in the cities of Verona, Venice, Bologna, Padua and Milan. In these cities they saw the works of the great Renaissance artists. This included works by the likes of Giotto, Titian, Bellini and Fra Angelico. They also saw the varying styles of architecture and cityscapes formed when Italy was made up small city states rather than being a unified nation. Regrettably, Oscar left his travelling companions before they went to Rome as he had, not unsurprisingly, run out of funds by this point. He returned to Ireland, for the remaining summer break to compose poetry inspired by his trip to Italy.

At the start of his second term Oscar returned to lectures wearing a new style of clothes, including high collars, check-print suits and neckties, while his once long hair had been cropped during the holiday period. Despite his hiccup regarding the responses exam, Oscar threw himself into the more social aspect of undergraduate life. Where there was merriment and fun, Wilde was often to be found, singing, betting and drinking. This lifestyle inevitably caused him to start a pattern that would continue until his death in 1900. He would become known for running up big debts in his pursuit of pleasure and fun. Oscar did attempt to turn his hand to rowing, that most Oxbridge of sports, but did not have either the dedication or the concentration, so this would be a very short-lived activity. Wilde and his circle were more likely to be found as spectators to various sporting events, rather than participants.

Upon his return to Magdalen, Oscar found he had been upgraded in his campus accommodation. His new student rooms were situated on the ground floor of the pretty cloisters of the college, with views of the river from one of his windows. The interiors were no less grand than the location, as they were lined with oak panels giving that scholarly yet elegant sense of decor. Wilde would make the space his own by adding sketches of nudes, charming nick-nacks, a piano and two large and very ornate Sèvres-esq vases in blue.

To fulfil his role as the hospitable Irishman he also ensured that there were decanters and glassware for all types of drink – from soda tumblers, to port glasses. Once again, he was living outside of his comparatively modest means and accumulating debt. Just like his mother, Oscar would hold soirees and get-togethers in his student quarters so he and his friends could discuss varying topics of interest, as well as partake of gaming, gambling and general merry making. This often included singalongs with his piano.

Even though the university had strict rules pertaining to the students going to licensed premises within the city, it seems students of the nineteenth century, like students of today, are naturally drawn to such places. The students caught during Oscar's time at Oxford were reprimanded by the university law officers, the proctors, and Wilde was often fined for his defiance of this particular university rule.

On 23 February 1875, Oscar Wilde was initiated into the Apollo Lodge of the Freemasons, and by 25 May he had progressed to the point he could be invested as a Master Mason. One tradition of the Freemason which would have appealed to Wilde was their tradition of dressing up in black knee-length breeches, silk stockings, pumps with tail coats and white tie. Of course, another appealing aspect of joining the Freemasons was the banquets and dances they frequently held.

It was not all fun during that first term back in 1875. Oscar had managed to get one of his poems published in the confusingly entitled, *Dublin University Magazine*. The publication was affiliated with the Trinity College Dublin, but was actually written and read mostly in London. To get a poem published was quite an achievement as the journal had a history of publishing elite contributors including contributions from both of his parents.

There was a night of high jinks on 1 November 1875, which resulted in Wilde and his friends being barred from taking part in any of the festivities on Guy Fawkes night. This rather harsh punishment was due to their impertinence to several university proctors.

It was during this academic year that he became a member of a second Freemasons' lodge called The Churchill. With this new circle of friends, he grew close to one particular chap, David Hunter-Blair. Hunter-Blair had recently converted to Catholicism and Wilde was fascinated by how and why his friend had done this. Oscar would accompany Hunter-Blair to services and witnessed Cardinal Manning give a sermon at the inaugural mass at St Aloysius, a new Catholic church in Oxford. This interest in the Catholic church would find a place within his room's decor, as he added a small statuette of the Virgin Mary, along with a small picture of the then reigning Pope, Pius IX.

Ruskin returned to Oxford and gave more public lectures, which Wilde attended. It was through this series of talks that the theory of Aestheticism was brought to Wilde's attention. The idea of art being for art's sake, and also life for art's sake, seems to have really connected with the twenty-something Wilde. It was also during this time that Wilde discovered another highly influential writer and fellow resident of Oxford, the controversial Walter Pater.

Walter Pater was born in 1839 and would become a controversial essayist, fiction and non-fiction writer and art and literary critic. Educated by some of the best institutes of the Victorian age, first King's School Canterbury, before becoming an Oxford man studying at Queen's College in 1858. Like Wilde and Swinburne, the Renaissance was of great interest to Pater. He would stay on in Oxford upon graduating and became part of the Classics department, while writing both fictional and non-fictional work at the same time. He would also become a published essayist and critic. It is easy to see why Wilde was drawn to such a figure.

In 1873, Pater was a Don at Brasenose College. During that year he published *Studies in the History of the Renaissance*. This was made up of a collection of eight essays. In this work, Pater expresses that man should devote his life to finding and experiencing art. As Pater puts it, 'art comes to you frankly professing to give nothing but the highest quality to your moments as they pass, and simply for that moments sake'. (Pater, *Studies in the History of the Renaissance*) He had, for all sense and purposes, just written the manifesto for the Aesthetic Movement.

The most controversial part of the work was that it not only challenged Victorian conventions of religion, morality and scholarship, but the fact that it examined sexuality – particularly male homosexuality. The controversy would become worse when, in 1874, Walter Pater was at the centre of his own hushed-up homosexual scandal with an undergraduate student named William Money Harding. This scandal had happen the year before Wilde became a student at Oxford, but no doubt there was the usual gossip still floating around during Wilde's years in there. The scandal and notoriety of Pater would have appealed to Wilde.

Christmas 1875 was not a cheery affair in Dublin, as Oscar's father's health had started to decline. Despite the dreariness at home, Oscar started 1876 with another success, he had another poem published. His former mentor at Trinity, Robert Tyrrell, published Oscar's poem called 'The Rose of Love' in his journal *Kottabos*. This set a positive trend for 1876, as Oscar would be published several more times during that year.

Back in to the academic year, Wilde's social life at Oxford took over once again, though it would be a mistake to think he was not interested in doing well. The lights in Wilde's rooms were often seen glowing well into the early hours of the morning in order for him to keep up academically. His last term of that year was interrupted as he was called back to Dublin because his father was dying. Sir William Wilde died on the 19 April, 1876, and Oscar would remain in Dublin for the big public funeral that came with being a well-known public figure.

When he returned to Oxford, Oscar had become a property owner, having inherited four properties in Bray from his father. However, these properties would become nothing short of a millstone around Oscar's neck; unfortunately, like many of Sir William's properties, including Merrion Square, the four Bray houses were heavily mortgaged.

Wilde's hard work prior to leaving for Dublin would pay off when he returned to Oxford to sit his examinations in June 1876. While he waited to hear his results, Oscar and his circle of friends continued to enjoy life in Oxford. Endless rounds of lawn tennis, picnics, boating, merrymaking and flirting were indulged. The friends also took a a daytrip to Blenheim

Palace where, in the nursery of the palace, an 18-month-old Winston Churchill was residing.

The last of his educational commitments that academic year was his viva voce exam in July. Having enjoyed most of the last part of June with friends, Wilde returned to his lodging to prepare for his viva. This didn't start as smoothly as it could have done. On the day of the exam, 4 July, Oscar was to be woken up by a university clerk asking why he had not turned up for his oral exam. Wilde did take the exam and despite arriving late, he would prove his genius and not only pass with a first, but would come top of his year.

Wilde returned to Oxford for the academic year 1876/77. Despite his new financial problems due to the houses in Bray, he was not shy in spending what little money he had on non-essential extravagances. This included additional Masonic insignia on which he managed to run up a bill of £13. The items purchased included a sword, a belt, a sword strap, an embossed case, a collar and an apron.

Money was also spent on the decor of his rooms. His inspiration would come from John Ruskin and the Pre-Raphaelites who are considered the forerunners to the Aesthetic Movement. Wilde was not the only admirer of this style. Many financially comfortable and fashionable classes were using Morris & Company fabrics and a muted colour palette within their home decor. It was these muted, or secondary, colours and some grey carpeting that would be the backdrop to his growing collection of bric-a-brac and clutter. Surfaces were covered in pieces of decorative china, art works, both framed and unframed, as well as various pieces of functional glassware that would be used when he held his Sunday soirees. These pieces of glassware included Venetian hock glasses, various decanters and champagne glasses. All items not usually associated with students. It was also during one of these soirees that Wilde is said to have made one of his most prophetic statements about himself. It is said that when asked what his ambitions would be after Oxford, Oscar exclaimed: 'I'll be a poet, a writer, a dramatist. Somehow or other I'll be famous, and if not famous, I'll be notorious.' There has never been confirmation that Wilde did in fact utter these words, though they have gone down in Wildean mythology.

Before returning to Dublin for Christmas, Wilde headed to London to partake of all the fun of the season, including seeing *Macbeth* at the Lyceum theatre, where the notable Victorian actor Henry Irving took the lead role. Oscar was dazzled by his performance.

Having already done several years at Trinity and then undertaken undergraduate studies at Oxford, Wilde was starting to lose interest in his lectures. He was also starting to gain a reputation with the Dons for being a rebel against authority and a bit of a bad influence. He continued to get fines from the proctors for late night adventures and drinking.

One particular incident really put him out of favour with his college. In March 1877, when he was in the hall for an examination, each of the students would be called up to the front of the whole college. When it was Oscar's turn and he was stood at the front of the hall, the president of the college asked one of his tutors – Mr Allen, the Roman history tutor – how he found Wilde as a student. To which Allen was said to have replied, 'Mr Wilde absents himself without apology from my lectures, his work is most unsatisfactory.' The president addressed Wilde after hearing this saying, 'that is hardly the way to treat a gentleman Mr Wilde'. This was too good a chance to be smart in front of his peers and Oscar indulged in some cheeky naughtiness. He replied to the college president, 'But Mr President, Mr Allen is not a gentleman.' Wilde was subsequently asked to leave the hall. (Sturgis, *Oscar* p.100)

Wilde further fell out of favour with the college after the easter break when he took himself travelling to Greece and Italy. Details of this adventure can be found in the next chapter. Due to his adventures in Greece and Italy he would be extremely late for the start of the summer term of 1877. When he decided to return from his travels, Wilde had clearly been expecting his welcome from the college to be warm. Instead, the college authorities were far from impressed at his unauthorised extended sojourn, regardless of the fact that it was closely related to his studies. They decided in his absence to suspend his study until the following academic year, and he was penalised half of the money from his demyship, which was the sum of £47.50 (approximately £2,950 in today's money). A demyship is a scholarship fund at Magdalen College;

the word derives from the Latin 'demi-socii', meaning 'half-fellow'. This in turn refers to the sum of the scholarship money – half the amount awarded to full fellows. Oscar was also issued work to undertake before returning for the next academic year in October. Wilde was far from impressed, and he was not the only one unimpressed with the college authorities' ruling. Mahaffy, with whom he had travelled and who was a Don at Trinity, as well as Oscar's mother were both outraged at what they saw as an injustice against him.

As he had unexpected time on his hands, Oscar decided to indulge in a few fun weeks in London with friends to cheer himself up. Among his many social engagements, Wilde attended the summer exhibition at The Royal Academy of Art and the opening of a new gallery in town, the Grosvenor Gallery on Bond Street. Compared to the Royal Academy, the Grosvenor was very modern and perfectly encapsulated the change within art during the 1870s. It could have been an Aesthetic temple, and Wilde was among those invited to its opening. Many of the artists exhibiting at the Grosvenor Gallery were either members of, or were influenced by, the Pre-Raphaelite Brotherhood. Among those showing at the opening were works by John Everett Millais, Walter Crane, James McNeill Whistler and Edward Burne-Jones.

The pre-opening, private viewing of the gallery was held on 30 April 1877, and it included a Victorian list of the fashionable who's who's in art and society. This was an excellent place for an ambitious, charming witty Oscar Wilde to find himself. It was at this event that Wilde made acquaintance with James McNeill Whistler, who in turn was in the company of the rising star of the Whig party, and future Prime Minister, William Gladstone. Not long after this dazzling event, Wilde returned to Dublin.

Once back in his home city, Wilde did not brood over the fact he was not at Oxford; indeed, he threw himself into literature and intellectual pursuits before the summer started. One of the first things he did was organise to give a series of lectures at Alexandra College, an institute for young bright women of the city. As summer started, so did the social events that go with the season. Oscar spent an enjoyable summer season writing, playing tennis, shooting and socialising around Ireland. Needless to say, the required work set by his Oxford college was neglected and not completed.

Life for the Wildes was about to be struck by more misfortune. Sir William's illegitimate son Henry Wilson had always been warmly welcomed into the Wilde family and was thriving in his career at St Mark's Hospital. The family had been facing ever increasing financial difficulties since Sir William's death, due to the huge debts he had accumulated. Henry disliked seeing his father's family struggling, so he was willing to help them by buying the family home at Merrion Square, and allowing Lady Wilde to reside in the house for her lifetime. It was a very generous offer. But before the legalities could be finalised, Henry died suddenly. He was only 38. More surprises were to come as a result of Henry's premature death. In his last will it was assumed that his wealth would be split evenly between both of his half-brothers, Willie and Oscar. Instead, Willie inherited £2,000, while Oscar received just £100 and Henry's half of the property at Illaunroe, which they had jointly inherited from their father. There was a caveat to this as well. Henry, despite living in a predominantly Catholic country, held strong views against the Catholic faith, and the fact that Oscar was exploring Catholicism and considering conversion to Rome, greatly upset his half brother. Therefore, Oscar would only receive these bequeathed gifts if he remained a Protestant. In a roundabout way, however, all was not lost. Henry did help save Merrion Place, as Willie used his inheritance to secure the Wilde family home.

Further legal tangles regarding the inherited houses at Bray arose. In September he was offered £2,800 for the properties from an acquaintance, Mr Quinn. Initially Wilde agreed to this offer, but upon consulting with his agents dealing with the lease and sale of the properties, Messers Battersby, he subsequently received a higher offer. Fairly, Wilde said that if he received formal written notification of the higher offer by 11am on 1 October he would happily agree to sell to the higher bidder. The deadline came and went and no formal notification was received, so he agreed to sell to Mr Quinn for £2,800. The problem started when

Messers Battersby claimed to have sent the formal written notification prior to 1 October. This higher bid was for an offer of £2,900, just £100 more than Mr Quinn's offer. The sale was halted and legal proceedings started. It was not the best way to end what had been an enjoyable summer.

Wilde returned to Oxford to start his fourth year that October. He had failed to complete the work the college had set him but through wit, charm, and no doubt because the college knew that Wilde was an exceptional student, the college decided to readmit him to complete his studies. However, he did not receive the forfeit part of his demyship fund. Further to the loss of this extra income, Wilde was chased by creditors unpaid from when he had left in April. Among those recalling debts was the jeweller who had crafted his Masonry regalia.

Wilde had not just had fun over the summer period away from Oxford, he had in fact had several articles printed. One of which was a review of the opening of The Grosvenor Gallery. In this review he name-dropped, and then sent the article to, Walter Pater. Much to Wilde's delight, Pater replied and suggested that they meet when Oscar was back in Oxford:

> Dear Mr Wilde
> Accept my best thanks for the magazine and your letter. Your excellent article on the Grosvenor Gallery I read with great pleasure; it makes me much wish to make your acquaintance and I hope you will give me an early call on your return to Oxford.
> I should much like to talk over some of the points with you …
> Very truly yours Walter Pater.
>
> Walter Pater to Oscar Wilde,
> 14 July 1877

Wilde mentions and includes a copy of Pater's letter to him in a letter he wrote to one of his college friends, William Ward. He notes, 'you won't think me snobbish for sending you this? After all, it is something to be honestly proud of.' (Oscar Wilde to William Ward, Merrion Sq 19 July 1877)

Upon his return to Oxford, Wilde lost no time in following up on Pater's letter and invited him to his beautifully decorated rooms at Magdalen. Needless to say, the meeting was a great success and Wilde had succeeded in cultivating a connection with one of his heroes.

Wilde also attended the open talks of John Ruskin who was once again back in the university city. He drank in all that Ruskin had to say, as well as studied the way in which Ruskin delivered his lectures. It must have been a euphoric and intellectually stimulating time for the ambitious Oscar Wilde.

It was more than just Wilde's intelligence and character that was evolving at this time, he had also added to his extravagantly decorated and adorned rooms to give them a more aesthetic feel. To the eclectic assortment of bric-a-brac he already had, he found additions from his travels at Easter from Greece and Italy. He had also taken several items from the Wilde family home in Merrion Square, including several pieces of china and a marble bust of the Pope. And, of course, there were always an abundance of fresh flowers in his rooms. Later in life Oscar would cultivate a notion that fresh flowers had a restorative effect on him during times of depression and illness. Flowers would also play a large role in the themes of his poetry.

Though back in the university, Wilde's time was taken up more with socialising than academic work. It is not really surprising, as this was his sixth year of university education and he must have started to feel bored of the routine and monotony of student life; he was evidently eager for the next chapter of his life.

Oscar had put in some time and effort over the summer break to compose an entry for the most prodigious poetry prize at Oxford; the Newdigate Prize. Among the former winners was John Ruskin no less, and Oscar was determined to enter. As luck would have it, the theme of that year's poem was the Italian Renaissance city of Ravenna, one of the cities in Italy that he had visited with Mahaffy. As well as the prestige of winning such a prize, there was the added incentive of prize money, worth £21.

During the summer he had worked on that poem, that he simply entitled 'Ravenna'. He would constantly review it and add what he considered the best lines from his other poems, incorporating them into this important poem. The Newdigate Prize was held once a year and the results would not be announced until the following June. On 10 June 1878, the winner was finally announced and Oscar had won the prestigious prize. The person who was most pleased of this success after Oscar himself was his mother, Lady Wilde.

> It is the first pleasant throb of joy I have had this year – how I long to read the poem – well after all we have genius ... I am proud of you and ... this gives you a certainty of success for the future ... Ever & Ever with joy & pride, your loving Mother.
>
> Telegram, Lady Wilde to Oscar Wilde,
June 1878

It was not just his mother who was proud of Oscar's achievements, his brother Willie informed all of the Dublin based press of his brothers achievements. It was a great triumphant moment in his young life.

Even though his tutors were unimpressed with his nominal and token contributions as a student, Wilde had no intention of failing any of his exams. Once again he could be found working hard and revising into the early hours of the morning. The written exams started on 1 June 1878. In true Wilde fashion, he put on a performance during the written exam, requesting extra paper within minutes of the start of the exam, and handing in his papers an hour before the exam finished. He then bragged to his fellow students that he had done little to no reading or preparation for the examinations. The exam season was concluded with his viva. When the results were published, Oscar Wilde had managed to achieve a double first and was the top of his year once again. Upon getting his double first, the college authorities reinstated the confiscated funds from his demyship. He would need to return the following semester to resit his Divinity exam and then he would be awarded his full degree.

His academic career as a student was coming to an end, and it was on a great high note.

When he returned in October 1878, Wilde had to take lodgings away from the college as he would not be there for the full year. For this semester he resided in the centre of Oxford at 71 High Street, his lodgings were above a pharmacy. He retook the failed divinity exam on 22 November and passed. He had graduated from Oxford with a double first and growing reputation as a poet. Things were looking up for Mr Oscar Wilde.

Oscar's time at Oxford was arguably a fundamentally important period in his life, a time when the evolution of the great persona of Oscar Wilde, the man, the writer, the wit, began, not to mention his links with aestheticism. It was good training ground for his future ambitions, as well as being an excellent opportunity to make important connections that would help him fulfil his ambitions and dreams.

ITALY AND GREECE

'Humanity takes itself too seriously.
It is the world's original sin. '
The Picture of Dorian Gray

Since his school days at Portora Royal, Oscar Wilde had been bewitched by the Classical world. From the history of the ancient civilisations, to the Classical languages of Greek and Latin, Wilde had soaked up all the information he could. This would continue as a student at Trinity and through his association with Rev. John Mahaffy and at Oxford. When opportunity arose during his time at Oxford to travel to these places, accompanied by John Mahaffy and his vast knowledge, Oscar agreed readily. In an age when travel took days not hours, using various modes of transport, together with the adventure and thrill of treading in the footsteps the greats of the Classical world, Oscar must have been rather excited.

The first of Oscar's trips to the Classical and artistic regions of Europe was in the summer break of 1875, when he joined Mahaffy and one of Mahaffy's students, William Goulding, on a trip to take in the wonders of Northern Italy. This trip took in Bologna, Venice, Padua, Verona and Milan.

The art and architecture of these cities enthralled Wilde with their treasures. He was also aware that he was in the process of following in the footsteps of the Romantic poets, Lord Byron, Percy Bysshe Shelley and John Keats. As a budding young poet himself, this must have felt like an artistic awakening, full of beauty, wonder and awe. Among the great building and places Wilde and his companions visited were the unique Venetian Gothic palazzos along the Grand Canal and around Venice. This architecture marries Venice's influences from the East and the wealth of the city's merchants. Oscar's joy of Venice's Basilica San Marco is recorded in a letter he wrote to his mother, while on this trip:

> The Church of San Marco is most gorgeous; a splendid Byzantine church covered with gilding and mosaics inside and out. The floor of inlaid marbles, of colour and design indescribable, and through the sinking of the undulates in big sweeping waves. Splendid gates of bronze, everything glorious.
>
> Oscar Wilde to Lady Wilde, Milan,
24 June 1875

Also while in the lagoon city, the party took a trip to one of the islands, to visit the monastery where Byron stayed when he was in Venice. When in Padua, they paid a visit to the house where Alighieri Dante, the famous Renaissance poet lived. This may well have had special meaning for Wilde, because his mother famously claimed kinship to the Italian poet.

While in the north of Italy the party took in art from many of Italy's and the Renaissance's greatest artists including, Fra Angelico, Veronese, Bellini, and of course, the great Titian. Wilde was said to have declared that Titian's depiction of the *Assumption of the Virgin*, located in the Basilica S. Maria Gloriosa dei Frari, in the Venetian lagoon, as his favourite picture in Venice. While in awe of much that he and his travelling companions witnessed, Wilde was somewhat less complimentary about Milan's Duomo. The grand cathedral church is located in the centre of the city. Oscar was said to have called the Metropolitan-Cathedral Basilica of the Nativity of Saint Mary a failure. These comments can be found in another letter to his mother dated 25 June 1875: 'The cathedral is an awful failure. Outside the design is monstrous and inartistic. The over-elaborated details stuck high up where no one can see them, everything is vile in it.'

Milian was to be the last stop on the trip for Oscar, as by June his limited funds had run out and he needed to return to Ireland as Mahaffy and Goulding travelled south to take in more of the romance of the Italian

Renaissance. This trip, however, had given him a taste of what treasures the rest of Italy had to offer, and the artistic and historic treasures to be seen beyond Italy and into the Classical past. This trip would influence his poetry and live on in his imagination until he could find a way back.

Wilde did not get a chance return to Italy, or experience these great wonders of Classical world, including Greece, until 1877. During his Easter break from Magdalen in 1877, Wilde found himself, like many other students at that point in the academic year – short on ready funds. He had been hoping to join his friends, Ward and Hunter-Blair on a trip to Rome for the Easter break. Hunter-Blair telegrammed Wilde from Monte Carlo saying that he would place several bets, and if he won, then Oscar could use the winnings to join his friends. Luck was on Hunter-Blair's side, and Wilde received a message to say that his friend had won £60 in the casino. In 1877 £60 was no small sum. Wilde rushed to London where he was fortunate enough to meet Mahaffy, and his previous travelling companion, William Goulding, with a third chap named George Macmillan. Macmillan belonged to the established publishing family of that name. The trio were also heading to the Continent and Wilde was invited to join their party. The plan was that Wilde would initially travel as far as Genoa with them.

Oscar confided to his new travelling companions that one of the reasons he was heading to Rome, was to spend Holy Week and Easter there, and to indulge in his growing curiosity of the Catholic Church right at its most important feast. Hunter-Blair was a recent Catholic convert and was hoping that Holy Week in Rome would sway his friend Wilde to also convert.

Rev. Mahaffy, being of Protestant faith, was naturally horrified upon hearing that this was Wilde's agenda. He used the journey to attempt to dissuade his former student from both the Roman faith and visiting the city – especially during Holy Week. By the time the group of travelling companions reached Genoa, Wilde had been fully persuaded to continue with them on their journey to see and experience the wonders of Greece. Being a Classicist and a Greek speaker, it must have been easy enough to pursued the amenable Wilde to continue with them, despite his plans with Ward and Hunter-Blair. On this trip they experienced and saw many of the great sights that Wilde would have read about in his years of Classical studies.

On Good Friday 1877, the party of four, including Wilde, travelled to the now UNESCO World heritage site of Ravenna, situated on the north-eastern side of the Italian peninsula. The former city state, which is connected to the Adriatic sea via the Candiano Canal also known as the Canal Corsini, would leave a great impression on Oscar Wilde. He would use those memories to create his award-winning poem 'Ravenna' in 1879. From the Byzantine marvels of Ravenna, the party moved on down the eastern coast to the port of Brindisi – which is still the main ferry termini between Italy and Greece today. Oscar was voyaging to see the places he had studied at school and at two universities; to actually see where the history happened, and to hear the Greek language spoken by living Greeks, as well as to walk where the heroes of his Greek studies had walked.

Their ferry brought them to the island of Corfu. It was then that Wilde decided that he should write to Magdalen College explaining where he was and that he would be late back for the last semester of that academic year. After all, wasn't he experiencing and seeing the Classical world in the flesh. Surely this was as enriching as any lectures on the history, society, literature or languages of that Classical period of the past. Unfortunately for Oscar, Magdalen College did not agree with his reasoning on this matter. Oscar also wrote to Reginald Harding at this time explaining his change of plans:

> I never went to Rome at all! What a changeable fellow you must think me, but Mahaffy my old tutor carried me off to Greece with him to see Mycenae and Athens. I am awfully ashamed of myself but I could not help stand will take Rome on my way back.
>
> Postcard from Oscar Wilde in Corfu
> to Reginald Harding,
> 2 April 1877

From Corfu the party travelled to mainland Greece. They arrived in time for the Greek Orthodox Church's Easter, and so the party found themselves experiencing Holy Week for the second time in two weeks.

They made their way to the Peloponnese and for eight days they visited various archaeological digs and temples. Some of the wonders that they saw included the Greek theatre at Argos, Mycenaean ruins and Olympia. They finally reached Athens on 13 April 1877.

Both Wilde and Macmillan were ecstatic to have travelled and made their way to the cradle of civilisation and this would become the highlight of the trip for them both. They briefly ventured away from the Greek capital to take in the famous sites of Marathon and Academia. Having taken in as much as they could, the party departed Athens a week later on a steamer headed for Naples. It was at Naples that Wilde reluctantly took leave of his three travelling companions and headed towards Rome to meet up with Hunter-Blair and Ward in the Eternal City.

Oscar met his friends at their accommodation, Hotel d'inghilterre, which would also become Oscar's digs while he stayed in Rome. The three friends spent their time exploring the many ruins within the city as well as viewing the notable art and architecture on offer to the nineteenth-century traveller. However, Oscar's motivations were more spiritual than historical for this leg of his voyage, and his friend Hunter-Blair intended to monopolise upon these feelings and try and finally convert his Catholic-curious friend into the bosom of the Roman Church.

One of the biggest strategies used by Hunter-Blair to try to convert Oscar was to set up a private audience with the Pope through a connection that he had at the Vatican. Both Wilde and Hunter-Blair had a private audience with Pope Pius IX. During their meeting, the Bishop of Rome gave Wilde a blessing, placing his hands on the poet's head. During this benediction, Pius said that he hoped that Oscar would follow his friend's example and join the Catholic communion. Oscar Wilde would eventually make the commitment to convert to Catholicism twenty-three years later – on his deathbed in Paris.

There was also one other important stopping point on this personal pilgrimage, he insisted that he and his friends visit the non-Catholic cemetery in Rome, which is located near the city's old walls and the Pyramid of Cestius. Wilde wanted to visit the resting places of the poet John Keats (31 October 1795 – 23 February 1821) and his fellow Romantic poet and friend, Percy Bysshe Shelley (4 August 1792 – 8 July 1822). As he had already followed in Byron's footsteps in Greece (and Venice in his previous trip in 1875), it would have been important for Wilde to make this special pilgrimage to his poetic heroes' graves. Keats's grave in particular was of great interest to Wilde, as it has an unusual epitaph engraved upon it:

> This grave contains all that was the Mortal of a Young English Poet Who on his Death Bed, in Bitterness of his Heart at the Malicious Power of his Enemies Desired these words to be on his Tomb stone: Here Lies One Whose Name was Writ in Water.

Also in the non-Catholic cemetery there is a plaque also dedicated to Keats. Wilde was less impressed with this memorial, as he did not like the carved likeness on the plaque. His love of the poet won out and he got down and venerated the plaque, much to the embarrassment of his travelling companions.

This personal pilgrimage to see the Romantics' graves in Rome would written about in a letter Wilde wrote in May 1877 from Merrion Square to Lord Houghton:

> Someways standing by his grave I felt that he too was a martyr, and worthy to lie in the City of Martyrs. I thought of him as a Priest of Beauty slain before his time, a lovely Sebastian killed by the arrows of a lying and unjust tongue.

Later in that same letter Oscar describes how he disliked the memorial plaque erected to Keats in the same cemetery:

> What is really objectionable in it is the bas-relief of Keats head – or rather a medallion profile, which is extremely ugly, exaggerates his facial angle so as almost to give him a hatchet-face.

Reflecting on his travels, and particularly on his time in Rome with Hunter-Blair and Ward, Wilde found a certain *joie de vivre* in the fact that the Catholic headquarters at the Vatican had numerous depictions of Greek and Roman gods, as well as the expected images and statues of Christian iconography. Like every grand adventure, Oscar's travels did eventually need come to an end. As noted in the previous chapter, his return to Oxford in April 1877 saw him receive a suspension from Magdalen for the rest of that academic year. Before heading home to Dublin, Oscar enjoyed a few weeks in the bright light and culture of London.

These trips to Italy and Greece not only helped shape the Oscar Wilde that many of us think of today, they brought to life his love of the ancient Classical world – its culture, language and history. He was also able to follow in the footsteps of his more modern heroes, the Romantic poets of the previous century. His visit to the city of Ravenna would also have helped him win the prestigious poetry award, the Newdigate Prize. It was this poem and award that helped launch him as a poet.

His trip to the Vatican to meet the Pope could also be argued to have had a lasting and important impression on Wilde. Although he would not convert to the Catholic Church straight away, Wilde would convert at what many Catholics view as the most important time in life, the hours before we leave this moral realm and die. In this respect, Wilde reminds me of Charles II of England, who also converted to Rome upon his deathbed; in faith, it seems that both men felt the need to be political rather than personal in their spirituality for most of their lives.

These voyages of discovery happened at crossroads in Wilde's life, as he was coming to the end of his academic career and was about to venture out into the world. The poet, the writer, and the real Oscar Wilde was moulded on these trips to the past.

OSCAR WILDE AND THE AESTHETIC MOVEMENT

'All those who find beautiful meanings in beautiful things are the cultivated.'

Oscar Wilde

When we think of Victorian Britain, we have certain preconceived ideas; that it was a society rather prim, proper and straightlaced, with clear social-class distinctions, and high social and personal morals. Society was, by and large, hardworking and generally God-fearing, in a very Anglican way. For a movement such as Aestheticism (1860–1900) to have developed and evolved during this period, and gone on to thrive, is rather surprising; as Aestheticism goes against these traditional views of the Victorian period.

The English Oxford Dictionary's definition of Aestheticism is: 'Aestheticism: Noun. An approach to art and life based on the belief that art and beauty should be valued for themselves and not for social or moral purposes.'

In other words, Aestheticism is to view art 'for art's sake', and enjoy the beauty of it. It is easy to see how and why Oscar Wilde became the movement's poster boy; he embodied Aestheticism throughout his writing, especially his poetry. The movement and ideas can also be seen throughout other areas of his life, particularly how he dressed, how he lived and decorated his rooms at Oxford, and then again later, how he and Constance decorated their family home. All these behaviours and choices personify and depict the theory of Aestheticism faultlessly.

There are several aspects to the theory of Aestheticism, particularly regarding art in all forms (including writing, which is most relevant to Wilde). The Aesthetes, as the followers of the movement became known, strongly believed in their theory of Brain v Body. To satisfy the body we need to do practical things such as eat, wash, work in order to be able to keep a roof over your head, buy food etc. To satisfy the mind, we need to meet its artistic and intellectual needs. The Aesthetes believed that the needs of the body take away too much time, and that the needs of brain are greatly neglected. They hoped to redress this by how they chose to live, act, dress and behave. Already this means that this way of living can not be achieved by, or be widely accessible to, the majority of people, as most people needed to work for an income, thus had less leisure time to undertake intellectual and artistic satisfaction for the brain.

The Aesthetes also believed that beauty is the most important value by which to live your life. This should be expressed in what you do in life, be it in the words you write, the images you paint or the clothes you choose to wear. This, too, is problematic, as each of us have an individual and different perception of what beauty is. The Aesthetes get around this by using Classical world definitions of beauty, left to us in their statues and art as their guidelines to what is considered to be perceived as beauty. This is another aspect of the movement that would have appealed to Wilde, as a student and admirer of the Greek and Classical world.

However, the 'beauty' within art, regardless of its form, should not have needed nor required a social or moral agenda. This means that the Aesthetes merely saw art as beautiful or not, regardless of what the artist may have been trying to say with their pictures. An example in case would be an Aesthete looking at a piece of Renaissance art. To demonstrate this, take the famous image of Leonardo da Vinci's *The Virgin of the Rocks*. At face value, it is an enticing picture of two captivating women, conventionally beautiful, and their two cherubic young children. Superficially, it meets the requirements of Aestheticism in being beautiful. However, due to the subject of the painting it cannot just be seen as just art for art's sake. This is, of course, because it is an image of the Virgin Mary and her cousin Elizabeth, together with their sons, Jesus Christ and John the Baptist. Art historians can go further by analysing the symbolism of the positions of the Virgin Mary's hand, how her head is at a certain angel, the colours used by da Vinci to paint her clothes, the interaction of the children on the picture – the list goes on. Therefore, there is a message or an agenda within this beautiful image.

The idea of art for art's sake, and defining ideas of beauty, on the surface seems rather vain and superficial, considering only a small part of the potential of any piece of art. Indeed, for art to be art it doesn't even need to be beautiful, it can be moving and emotional, depicting images of death, violence and ugliness. Using these ideas, the Aesthetes would not have considered the works of Pablo Picasso, Salvador Dali, or even Caravaggio, worthy, and that seems very shallow and narrow minded.

Much of Oscar Wilde's poetry, and many of his plays, can be described as Aesthetic; however, his ultimate Aesthetic work is his only full novel, *The Picture of Dorian Gray*, published in 1890. Briefly, *The Picture of Dorian Gray* is the story of a painting, its muse and the artist and their friends. The artist, Basil Hallward, is in the process of painting a portrait of his latest muse, Dorian Gray, a beautiful youth. Hallward is in love with Gray's beauty. Lord Henry Wotton, one of Hallward's friends, has aesthetic sensibilities and has a bad influence over Dorian Gray whom he meets at Hallward's studio. Flattered by the adoration and attention of Wotton, Dorian bargains his soul for eternal youth, asking that the signs of his ageing appear upon Hallward's portrait instead of himself. With no soul, Dorian goes on to carry out various cruel acts causing his victims to commit suicide as well as going on to kill the artist of his ageing portrait, Basil Hallward. Eventually his guilt causes him to destroy his portrait with a knife. His body is later discovered beside the destroyed painting; it is the body of an old man, stabbed to death...

This book is essentially a novel about art, culture and artists. By writing upon such themes, Wilde is expressing that it is a work of Aestheticism, and that his work is the superior judgement upon these ideas and themes. Through how he chooses to use language and certain words, he is setting this standard high. This is also achieved through the characters' various dialogues on the subject of art, beauty and culture throughout the story. The work itself is Aesthetic as it provides the reader with pleasure, through the beauty of Wilde's prose, which is in turn written to depict Aestheticism through the characters and themes. It can also be argued that through the story of *The Picture of Dorian Gray*, Wilde presents the arts as the highest form of human achievement, accomplishment and aspiration.

This is apparent in chapter two, when Dorian Gray is looking at his portrait:

> 'How sad it is!' Murmured Dorian Gray with his eyes still fixed upon his own portrait. 'How sad it is! I shall grow old and horrible, and dreadful. But this picture will remain always young. It will never be older than this particular day in June … If it were only the other way! If it was I to be always young and the picture that was to grow old! For that – for that – I would give anything! Yes there is nothing in the whole world I would not give! I would give my soul for that.'

The novel depicts Aesthetic materialism. Aestheticism can be expressed through surrounding oneself with objects that bring pleasure, joy and beauty, rather than have utilitarianism or bring function to one's life. These ideas mirror the new rising consumer culture happening at this time in Victorian Society. The industrial revolution was at its height during the reign of Queen Victoria and a new social class had emerged. Men from lower-classes had been given the opportunity to better themselves and through the industrialisation of many trades, a wealthy middle class with working-class origins emerged – many of whom were more affluent than the aristocrats and traditional upper-classes. This new class of people found they had both wealth and time, and could therefore explore art culture and other intellectual pursuits. They were materialistic, and brought art and beautiful things for their homes as a way to display their wealth.

It is often thought that Wilde represents himself through the central character of Lord Henry, who is dominant throughout the book, and his interests through the book's many discourses on themes of art culture and beauty. However, Wilde counters this notion in a letter written to Ralph Payne on 12 February 1894:

> I am so glad you like that strange coloured book of mine; it contains much of me in it. Basil Hallsword is what I think I am: Lord Henry what the world thinks me: Dorian Gray what I would like to be – in other ages perhaps.

The moral of *The Picture of Dorian Gray* is, perhaps, that Aestheticism is not a viable or a sustainable life choice. Arguably, the end to Wilde's own life and story, as he died in poverty and exile in Paris, would become the ultimate embodiment of the moral of this dark examination of Aestheticism.

However, where Oscar Wilde really embodied, and led, the Aesthetic Movement is through his life choices, dress and behaviour. Wilde thrived in going against the Victorian stereotypes mentioned in the introduction. By doing so, he turns Aestheticism into a lifestyle choice, as well as an art movement. He was also careful of his appearance, following fashions and trends while also setting new ones by interrupting the styles and dress codes of the Victorian era.

The Victorian man of Oscar Wilde's class dressed to unspoken social expectations and standards of etiquette. Everyday wear in the early Victorian period for men usually involved full black frock coat with tails, accompanied by a waistcoat. During the daytime, lighter coloured trousers were acceptable, however it would not be considered polite to wear lighter trousers to dinner or evening events. Trousers had evolved to have flies for convenience by this period and breeches were kept for formal dress events. The gentleman's shirt was usually made of either cotton or linen and typically white in colour. Shirt collars evolved and changed during this period. By 1850, gentlemen's collars were either high, so that you could see the tie around the neck and a small amount of collar above the tie, or something that we would recognise today as dress shirt collars that turned down over the tie around the neck.

Ties were worn as everyday wear, and could be interchanged with a cravat depending on time of day and social situation. The tie also evolved during Victoria's reign. By the 1860s the girth of the tie had become wider, allowing different ways to fasten and knot them. This wider tie allowed a gent to fasten their neckwear into bows or various knots, including the Ascot knot, the Windsor knot or the four-in-hand knot, which is still commonly used today by those who require a tie as part of a uniform such as school children and corporate workers.

The type of coat and Jacket did evolve and relax as the period went on. By the 1880s tuxedos were considered smart enough for evening dress, while blazers had been socially accepted as suitable leisurewear for situations such as going to a sporting event as relaxed alternative. The colour palette at the beginning of the period was mostly black, but as the period went on other darker colours were accepted and could be worn in accessories such as ties. Hats were expected to be worn by men of all social classes. The upper classes preferred to favour top hats as their headwear of choice, while lower-class men donned bowler hats or flat caps as their accepted head covering.

With regard to hair styling, the Victorian gentleman general chose to wear his hair in shorter styles, compared to earlier periods. There were several options open to the distinguished gentleman concerning facial hair, including prominent sideburns and full beards, generally favoured by the older gentlemen, while younger men generally preferred moustaches.

These social expectations were to be followed, regardless of the weather – for example those who went to work throughout the vast British Empire, in places such as India or Africa, were still expected kept the same standards, regardless how uncomfortable they would have been in the extreme heat.

It is easy to see how Oscar changed these dress-codes with his aesthetic style and flare. He often wore a cape, and he mixed up the materials used to make his garments – including fur or velvet for a more luxurious feel and display. He tended to mostly keep his hair longer than the average Victorian male, and his face was generally clean shaven. He would accessorise with flowers in his buttonhole - most famously the green carnation which would be adopted by many Victorian gay men. When it came to hats, Wilde shunned the traditional options of a top hat, bowler or flat cap, instead opting for a fedora with a wide brim and worn at a jaunty angle. All these fashion choices made by Wilde would become synonymous with the Aesthetic Movement.

It wasn't just the codes of men's fashion that were being broken by the Aesthetic Movement – women's clothing also evolved and even got its own movement and society, partly due to the influence of the Aesthetic Movement.

Until the mid-nineteenth-century, acceptable female dress was highly structured and uncomfortable to the point of being a health hazard. Outwardly the clothes were modest, plain and greatly impractical in many ways. For many women, getting dressed before the reforms started was like an Olympic sport and often required help from another person, especially women of a high social class. There would be several layers, structured corsetry, petticoats and hoops that were not only uncomfortable, but also heavy to wear. These features of female dress were not just to cover the body modestly, but also reflected a woman's morality, social standing and class. The Rational Dress Movement, also known as The Victorian Dress Reform Movement, aimed to make women's clothing more comfortable and practical for everyday living in an ever-modernising society. As well as being practical, the aesthetic part of the movement also wanted the new dress code to be beautiful as well as utilitarian.

These changes were not just due to the Aesthetic Movement, they were part of a bigger shift in attitude towards women in the later part of the Victorian era in Britain and Ireland. It was the dawn of the bigger feminist movements that worked towards the inclusion of women in the modernising world. The fact that they were being reigned over by a Queen and Empress, no doubt helped the movement find confidence to start – Victoria was a modern woman in some ways as she was fulfilling a traditionally male role and balancing motherhood with her work.

One of the first ways that the movement changed women's dress was not only discreet but it was liberating – the movement revolutionised women's underwear. This became known as 'emancipating waists'. Corsets were swapped for 'liberty bodices' – an early forerunner to the modern bra; not only were they less restrictive, they were fastened from the front, meaning women could dress themselves unaided.

The change to outer garments were intended to be of a looser fit than early Victorian clothes. They were intended to embellish the natural form and curves of a woman's body – the exact opposite to the corseted figure-fitting clothes in the earlier part of the nineteenth century.

The styles and shapes of the garments took inspiration from the medieval Romanised period and Renaissance, from the necklines to the sleeve styles. Womenswear which previously had been plain and in sombre colour palettes were now being made in dyed colours and enhanced with decorative embroidery. These enhancements can be seen to have been influenced and inspired by the growing Pre-Raphaelite Brotherhood, who were also closely linked to the Aesthetic Movement. These changes were mostly welcomed by women and by 1881, when the Rational Dress Society was established in London. Both Oscar and and his wife Constance supported their aims and work, and Constance became their unofficial model, often wearing these new styles of dress when out and about with Oscar during the early part of the marriage.

Oscar also expressed his aesthetic taste through the way he decorated where he lived. We have seen how he curated a maximalist interior to his university room at Oxford while he was a student. It was during this time that he had started to live beyond his means – a habit he continued even when he was at the height of his success and up until his impoverished death in 1900. His rooms at Magdalen College were decked out with frippery and nick-nacks, art and flowers, and all the things he needed to play the best host – from sherry glasses and decanters to a piano.

This style continued when both he and Constance styled their marital home. Prior to their marriage, Oscar and Constance found a home in Chelsea, a part of London that Oscar was keen to return to. The home was a newly built on Tite Street, then number 16. But the pair were not going to just move in to this conventional Victorian house; they had to redesign it to fit their aesthetic lifestyle. After all Oscar had toured America lecturing on that very subject, it would not have done to live in a traditional conservative London terrace house.

Oscar and Constance married on 29 May 1884, and upon returning from their honeymoon, their new home was not finished. It still was not finished at Christmas of that year, though they moved in and continued their aesthetic makeover while in residence. The lower floor of the house had been decorated by E.W. Godwin, with the help and advice of Wilde's artist friend, James Whistler. However, the upper floors were decorated by Wilde and Constance. In his autobiography, the Wildes' youngest son Vyvyan describes the eclectic different styles that made up the family home until 1895. According to Vyvyan, the first floor was covered in art from the Pre-Raphaelites and etchings by Whistler, decorated with Japanese wears such as vases, and that the walls were yellow in colour.

Vyvyan also describes his father's Smoking Room as gloomy. It had been decorated with Lincrusta-Walton wallpaper in dark red and gold in a William Morris pattern. The additional decor was North African themed and it was lit by Moroccan lanterns. Visitors to the smoking room were expected to lounge and recline upon divans and ottomans. This description of the smoking room, evokes a sensual and exotic atmosphere – the smoke making it even more alluring. The use of William Morris patterns throughout the house is a nod to the Arts and Crafts Movement that Oscar loved so much; it very much reflects his tastes and eccentric flamboyancy.

One of Oscar Wilde's best-known quotes about aestheticism is: 'It is through Art and Art only we can realise our perfection; through Art and Art only that we can shield ourselves from the sordid perils of actual existence.' This once again proves that the Aesthetic Movement, particularly the lifestyle aspect, could only really be realistically followed by those who were fortunate enough to not need to work in order to survive in body and soul. The true aesthete required time to allow them to focus on beauty, art, learning and pleasurable pursuits – a luxury few could afford. In truth, Wilde himself could not really afford to live like this full time, particularly after he married and started a family with Constance. But financial responsibility was never one of Oscar's strengths and keeping up aesthetic appearances was far more important to him than a pension pot.

The Victorian Christian view encouraged living this life well by working hard and by upholding Christian moral and values in order to be rewarded in the next life. Aestheticism, however, could be seen as having anti-Christian undertones; Aesthetes followed a much more modern way of viewing life, believing that you only live once so it is imperative that you should enjoy it, take pleasure in it, seek beauty in it.

The ideas of the Aesthetic movement can be seen in other movements that were formed around this time, most notably the Pre-Raphaelites in Britain, and Art Nouveau and the work of the Avent Garde movement in Paris.

Pre-Raphaelite Brotherhood were a group of seven students and friends who shared the same ideas on life and art. They were: William Holman Hunt, John Everett Millais, James Collinson, Frederic George Stephenson, Thomas Woolner and the Rossetti brothers – William Michael and Dante Gabriel.

Although the original brotherhood had disbanded by 1854 – the year of Wilde's birth in Dublin – the brotherhood had acquired disciples that continued their ideas through their own works. These evolved ideas turned it into other movements in art and the new followers included: Ford Madox Brown, Arthur Hughes, John William Waterhouse, Edward Burne-Jones, William Morris and, arguably, much later on, Oscar Wilde himself.

Both the Pre-Raphaelite Brotherhood and the Arts and Crafts Movement wanted simpler way of being, through how they lived, dressed and their art. Both ideologies had rebellious, almost anti-establishment undercurrents to them. Both movements also held beauty as an important ideal to their doctrines; it is easy to see how some of the early ideas of Aestheticism grew from the Pre-Raphaelite Brotherhood. These ideas were then developed and refined even further by Dante Gabriel Rossetti in what became Aesthetic Pre-Raphaelitism. Another related movement that evolved from the Pre-Raphaelites was the Arts and Crafts Movement, which was greatly admired and revered by Oscar. Dante in particular inspired poet Algernon Charles Swinburne. Swinburne in turn was a great influence upon Wilde's early poetry after they met and he read Swinburne's works during his Oxford days.

The biggest difference between the two ideologies was that unlike the aesthetes, Pre-Raphaelite art was more than just beautiful, it was full of meaning and symbols much more akin to works from the Renaissance.

Oscar was able to meet several prominent members of the Arts and Crafts Movement that were inspired by the Pre-Raphaelites, most notably Edward Burne-Jones and William Morris. Burne-Jones and Wilde became good friends, often entertaining at either Tite Street or the Grange, Burne-Jones's home, located in West Kensington. Burne-Jones, who was naturally prone to be of a morose disposition, found Wilde's wit a tonic that would leave him laughing out loud.

It was through Burne-Jones that Wilde got to meet one of his childhood heroes, the prominent member of the Arts and Crafts Movement, William Morris. They first met in the spring of 1881, and Morris was less than impressed upon his first acquaintance with Wilde. Morris though Wilde was clever but a bit of an ass. Thankfully, subsequent meetings changed Morris's opinion of Wilde, when he went on to describe Wilde as 'uncommonly good company'.

Oscar Wilde also lived during another movement closely associated with Aestheticism. It was very popular in Western Europe, particularly Paris, France and Belgium. It was the Art Nouveau movement and lasted from 1888 until 1900. Nothing could be just be utilitarian, everyday items – from drain covers and drainpipes, to the interiors of public toilets, to door knockers and door frames – were all highly decorated in nature-inspired motifs. Just like Aestheticism; it was modern, but also very beautiful. One of the most lasting and iconic uses of the Art Nouveau movement can be seen at the entrance of many of Paris's metro stations. The metro that opened during the last few months of Oscar's life while he was living in the French capital.

Arguably, the Aesthetic movement is an important factor in creating the story of the *real* Oscar Wilde. He strove to embody the ethos of the movement through his works, his dress, how he decorated his living spaces, how he used language in his writing and speech, and in his general way of life.

Oscar's Tour of North America, 1882

'America is the only country that went from barbarism to decadence without civilisation in between.'

Oscar Wilde

Having triumphed at Oxford and already gained a taste of the fame that would come later on, Oscar Wilde was now itching to get out into the real world and grow and build on his successes and reputation. His time at Oxford had allowed him to sharpen and hone his whimsical wit, repartee and banter. After successfully being published as a poet the previous year and gaining minor celebrity status, Oscar was featured in the satirical journal *Punch*. He needed to find a way to capitalise on this publicity and start earning a living. The question was, how could he earn a living while maintaining his aesthetic lifestyle and image?

Earlier in 1881 it had been suggested to Wilde, by several friends and acquaintances, that he should undertake a speaking tour of the United States. To start with, Wilde was not very keen on the idea, but as 1881 progressed and his poetry became successful in the US, and Aestheticism started to become known about, Wilde warmed to the idea. In late September 1881, a promoter based in New York who organised lecture tours across the States telegrammed Wilde enquiring whether he was interested in undertaking such a tour. On 1 October, Oscar replied to this telegram that yes, if the deal was right, he was interested in lecturing on Aestheticism in the United States and Canada. The promotor in question was Richard D'Oyly Carte, and his business associate Colonel Morse. Carte and Morse had experience in arranging such speaking tours around the US and colonies. They wanted to build on the growing interest in the States towards Aestheticism.

Negotiations with D'Oyly Carte and Morse started in October 1881 and while that was going on in the background, Oscar turned his hand to composing the talks he wanted to present. The topics he had wanted to lecture on were entitled: 'Beauty as seen in everyday life', and 'The poetical methods used by Shakespeare'. D'Oyly Carte and his team were less enthusiastic about these ideas and persuaded him to shift the focus of his talks to themes of Aestheticism.

Eventually a deal between Wilde and D'Oyly Carte was struck, and the dates to start his tour were set for early 1882. As well as changing his lecture ideas, Oscar now had to decide upon his wardrobe, for it was essential that he was seen to be every inch the aesthete. Part of his costume for his aesthetic persona, would be his breeches from his masonic regalia. To this he added a fur coat, and he decided to wear his hair in a longer, more bohemian style and length.

On Christmas Eve 1881, Wilde boarded the SS *Arizona* and set sail for New York. The ship arrived during the evening of 2 January 1882. The passengers had to wait on board the *Arizona* until the following day before being allowed to disembark at Ellis Island, because the customs office was closed when they arrived.

As Wilde sailed across the Atlantic, both D'Oyly Carte and Morse had been busy promoting their new act, this meant that even before the passengers of SS *Arizona* had disembarked, there was a pack of New York press journalists and photographers waiting for Wilde. They were so desperate for the scoop of his arrival that many of the journalists and photographers were willing to take small boats close to the *Arizona* in order to shout out questions to the ship's star passenger, ahead of their press deadline for the morning papers. Their thirst for gossip led some of the more resourceful hacks to get quotes from Wilde's fellow passengers. One of whom told them they had walked with Wilde on the deck during the voyage. When Oscar was asked about the journey he had answered that he was 'unimpressed with the Atlantic and he wanted a storm'. Of course, it was this second-hand comment that was quoted and would make the headlines of the morning papers. This first encounter with the US press was a sharp learning curve for the Dublin boy who had previously only dealt with mild humour from British publications. He quickly realised that they craved quotable and witty phrases for their copy and headlines. Thankfully, this first headline worked in Oscar's favour and was seen to show that he had a sense of humour.

Finally, on the 3 January 1882, as he disembarked in New York, legend has it that Oscar Wilde is meant to have said one of his most well known and quoted quips to a New York customs officer. The tale states that Wilde responded to the question 'have you anything to declare?' with the immortal line: 'I have nothing to declare, but my genius'. Sadly, there has never been any evidence to prove he did, indeed, utter those words. In fact, it may well have been Wilde himself that started that rumour after the event, while retelling his US adventures back at home. Upon arriving in New York, D'Oyly Carte and Morse suggested that Oscar made his social debut by attending the opera in full Aesthetic dress so that he could be seen by the cultured people. The operatic audience would be his target audience and the demographic who would be willing to pay to hear a talk given by Wilde. The idea was to be seen and to generate a buzz – a publicity trick still used today in the twenty-first century, ahead of a premier or product launch.

Even in the late nineteenth century, New York was already a towering city of skyscrapers, many of which were still in construction. This cityscape must have been awe inspiring to the Dublin-born poet. Even the Victorian New Yorkers were always rushing and hustling, making both London and Dublin seem like small towns in comparison.

Wilde had arrived a full week before his first advertised talk was to take place, and for most of that week, D'Oyly Carte and Morse had set about keeping Wilde in the public eye while still attempting to maintain an air of mystery around him. One way they achieved this was to have Wilde travel around the city in a carriage, this was so that he could be seen and generate interest due to his unique aesthetic fashion style. Oscar was also advised to pay a visit to Mrs Frank Leslie, an influential widow and the owner of five US newspapers. Naturally, Wilde was able to charm her, and subsequently gained the support of her publications in doing so.

In those first few days many of the interviews given by Wilde focused on Aestheticism and art rather than about him as a person. As D'Oyly Carte and Morse did their job, and interest grew in Oscar, it was getting harder for him to have any privacy. D'Oyly Carte et al decided it would be better to rent a short-term lease apartment for him in New York, rather than continue to stay in hotels. Wilde settled into his temporary home on 28th Street, however the privacy did not last long. One of the journalists that came to interview him in his apartment subsequently published Wilde's full address in the *New York Star*. Despite the disruption and general hubbub of the city, Oscar was able to finish and refine his talk between interviews.

D'Oyly Carte and Morse also used a newer form of marketing – they sold the use of Wilde's image. They had photographers bidding to take pictures of Wilde and had exclusive rights to for their use for the duration of his tour. They made their money back by selling these official images to publications and for advertising purposes. Anyone not using the official images to illustrate their articles would be sued.

D'Oyly Carte and Morse chose Napoleon Seroni the same photographer that took the images of Oscar's friend Sarah Bernhardt. Seroni was a great choice, he was a quirky and unique individual known for his big moustaches and fez hats. Wilde went to his studio on 5 January 1882, and the pair created images of Wilde that encapsulated the Aesthetic style perfectly. Seroni paid $1,500 for the exclusive use of Wilde's image, This was a large sum in 1882, for the images of a relatively unknown breakthrough Irish poet.

The invitations to social events and dinners held in his honour by the cultured literati of the Big Apple, keep coming. Many of these events would have been very similar to those his own mother had held during his childhood in Dublin. One of the most prestigious of these was held by Mrs D.G. Crowley. She was better known by her *nom de plume*, Jenny June. Wilde found himself the joint literary guest with the

American novelist Louisa May Alcott, author of the American classic, Little Women.

The first of Oscar's lectures was held at the Chickering Hall, located on the corner of 5th Avenue and West 18th Street. The talk was simply entitled, The English Renaissance, the venue sold all its 1,000 tickets at 1$ each. In true Wilde style, Oscar started his talk to his packed out and eager audience ten minutes fashionably late.

The talk was not what we traditionally picture, when we think of Oscar Wilde. It was serious, academic and abstract. It would not have been out of place in a university lecture hall. After a nervous and somewhat awkward start, Wilde eventually won his audience over with his trademark humour. The atmosphere relaxed and the rest of the talk was a triumphant success. At the closing line of his speech, stating 'the secret to life is art', the audiences broke out in enthusiastic applauds. And so Oscar Wilde had started to become New York's newest favourite celebrity.

It was not just the audience that loved his talk, the press cuttings were primarily enthusiastic too. With New York a firm success, the rest of Wilde's tour was publicised. This new-found fame also required for Oscar to employ two secretaries to answer his fan mail. One of these poor men found himself donating locks of his own hair to meet the demands from young women wanting a cutting of Oscar's hair.

Another positive effect of his success in New York was that his first volume of poetry published the year before in 1881, ended up going into additional prints in 1882. Wilde had hoped, his new popularity would help him to get some Broadway interest in his play, *Vera*. With this first success under his belt, Oscar left New York riding high on his success as he headed to the next US city on his tour, Philadelphia, Pennsylvania.

The Philadelphia publication, *Our Continent* was particularly pleased that Mr Oscar Wilde was coming to their city. Prior to leaving London for the US, *Our Continent* had contacted Oscar and commissioned two poems from him ahead of his tour. Oscar completed these two poems during his first week in New York. The two twelve verse poems were called, 'Le Jardin' and 'La Mer'. 'Le Jardin' (The Garden) was all about the two iconic flowers associated with Aestheticism, the sunflower and the lily. The second poem 'La Mer' (The Sea) was an ode to the sea at night. No doubt he was inspired by his own transatlantic crossing to the States. The proprietor of *Our Continent*, Robert S. Davis, welcomed Wilde to the city with a reception held in his honour. Davis was not Oscar's only connection to the city, as he had a second cousin based in Philadelphia, Fr Basil Martin, an Irish-born Anglican Protestant who had relocated to the US, like many Irish in the mid-nineteenth century due to poverty and the great potato famine that struck the Irish potato crop between 1845–49.

Oscar made the Aldine hotel his base while he stayed in Philadelphia. Soon, news of his awaited arrival caused him to be in even more demand; so much so, that Wilde had to station his valet, Traquair, outside his room to inform visitors that Mr Wilde wasn't available.

Wilde, on the whole, was fairly open-minded about many issues that others during the Victorian age still considered taboo. This included issues like women's dress reform and of course his defence of homosexuality. Therefore it is uncomfortable to discover that Wilde referred to his African American valet, Traquair as 'his slave' in a letter. Traquair was employed by Wilde for the duration of his US tour. Slavery had only been abolished twelve years before Wilde was there during 1882. Much of the country still treated African Americans and former slaves like second-class citizens (in reality, the change fought for in the American Civil War did not happen until the mid-twentieth century and is still a social issue in the States today). There is no evidence that he was cruel or disrespectful to Traquair in person, but given the animosity towards the Irish in the US, one would have hoped he would have been more empathetic towards the man he employed as his valet. The comment may have been meant flippantly or in humour rather than callously, but it makes for uncomfortable reading. Times and sensibilities change and things said in the past may have been more socially acceptable then, but it can still create an unpalatable account of historical characters.

On the evening of 17 January, when Wilde held his first talk in Philadelphia at the Horticulture Hall, once again he had managed to sell out all of the 1,100-seat auditorium. However, unlike New York the Philadelphians were less impressed with his talk. This must have felt like such an anti-climax for Oscar after his enthusiastic praise and reception in New York.

This disappointment was soon forgotten when Oscar got to meet one of his literary heroes in person, the US poet Walt Whitman. During the afternoon of 18 January, Whitman welcomed Oscar into his home and served some of his homemade elderflower wine, which Oscar later confessed he only drank due to his great admiration for Whitman, rather than liking it. The conversation between the two men was easy to come by and broached a number of subjects, including the work of Alfred Tennyson, beauty in all things, poetry, William Morris and the Rossettis. Both men thoroughly enjoyed their meeting.

Reflecting on their cooler reception in Philadelphia, Oscar decided that his lecture needed to be tweaked and reworked. This became even more pressing when a Mr George Monroe published an unauthorised copy of the lecture and sold it for 10c in his publication *Seaside Library Edition*. If people could get his talk for as little as 10c, they would not pay 1$ a ticket to see Wilde talk in person. The resulting changes saw Wilde take out about thirty minutes of the more academic theory that was in his lecture, as well as relaxing the style and tone of the language used. This new talk would be tried out in the next city on this tour, Washington DC.

Oscar was again welcomed warmly in Washington DC and he was once again in demand by the social literati. He would be met and greeted by senators and the British-American children's author, Frances Hodgson Burnett, who is best known *Little Lord Fauntleroy* (1886) and later *The Secret Garden* (1911) On 23 January, Wilde gave his new and improved talk at Lincoln Hall in Washington DC. Again, the reviews and audience response was mixed rather than triumphant, although all the press did agree that his talk was interesting; given that he had reworked the lecture however, Wilde must have felt a little disappointed. With fame there came the inevitable jealousy and negativity alongside the praise, both within social circles and in the press. While in Washington DC he was reacquainted with the American-British author, Henry James. Although Wilde was a fan of James, it was by no means a mutual feeling.

It is worth noting that in the US, Oscar was primarily billed as an 'English' poet rather than Irish. The whole of Ireland was of course considered part of the United Kingdom and the British Empire, Victoria was their queen and Ireland was still a united country. Therefore it may not have seemed quite as strange at first glance to see why he was publicised as 'English'. However, at this time – due largely the large influx of Irish immigrants on the back of the potato famine of the 1840s – there was widespread anti-Irish feeling in some of the bigger cities within the United States, especially cities where larger communities of Irish had settled, such as New York and Boston.

The next city on his tour brought him back up the coast to Baltimore. Here, he needed to charm the city even more as there had been a misunderstanding about when he was due to arrive. The problem was caused by miscommunication Wilde had been expected to stop off at Baltimore en route to the Washington DC. By all accounts he managed to charm them after he gave his talk to a sold-out audience of 800 on 26 January, at the city's Academy of Music.

From Baltimore Oscar returned to New York, to the Albany Music Hall, though he did not stay the night after giving his lecture on 27 January. The pace of the tour was picking up as he left on the midnight train to Boston following that lecture. Although he was now travelling a lot, Boston would give him one of the warmest welcomes on his tour. This was mostly due to the city's most high-profile literary society, 'The Saturday Club'. They issued an invitation to Wilde to be their special guest at their monthly luncheon. There were some notable names of American culture and literature within the club's membership. They included Ralph Waldo Emerson and Oliver Wendell Holmes – an author Wilde had become a fan of during his Oxford days. Sadly, Emerson was too infirm to make it to Wilde's special lunch.

Although he was unable to attend the lunch, Henry Wadsworth Longfellow did reach out to Wilde to meet while he was in the Boston area. Wilde was familiar with Longfellow's work and particularly admired and liked his translation of Dante. Wilde called to see Longfellow at his Boston home. Both men enjoyed the meeting and Longfellow described the young Irish poet as 'a very agreeable young man'. Unfortunately, it would not be a long-lasting friendship as Longfellow died about a month after he met with Wilde.

The Boston lecture took place on 31 January at one of the city's music halls. With Boston being home to the acclaimed Harvard University, a good proportion of Wilde's audience naturally came from the student body of the famous institution. The students decided to turn up to the talk in full Oscar Wilde costume, including knee breeches, stockings, and brandishing sunflowers. Not wishing to be outdone by the students, Wilde decided to wear a very conventional and conservative set of evening wear. He opened the speech by saying: 'Save me from my disciples'. This light note at the start of the lecture won the students and the rest of the audience over and it was a success. This talk completed the first of eleven months touring the United States and February was going to be no less busy.

In just a month, the East Coast of America had been taken under the spell of Oscar Wilde. Upon return to New York on the 3 February there were gentlemen's attire stores displaying their products with sunflowers and lilies, and describing their latest items as 'approved' by Mr Oscar Wilde. The florists of the city were struggling to source enough leonine sunflowers to meet the demand. The most produced image on trading cards in 1882 was of Oscar Wilde.

What was most bizarre was that Oscar's image was also used to advertise all sorts of products, the majority of which he may have not been aware of – or even approved of, had he known. The strangest of which was 'Mme Maire Fountaine Bosom Beautifier'. This was a product that would will help increase the size and firmness of a woman's bust area. The product was suitable for women of more mature years as well as youthful ladies in order to correct bust sagginess. I am not sure what Oscar would have made of this product.

After a mostly successful first month lecturing in America, Oscar started to dream of great wealth. As he employed Carte & Co to manage and arrange the business side of the tour, any profits made had to be split as per the contract, which in this case was 50/50, however Oscar's personal expenses would come out of his half of the profits. There was great potential for Oscar to return to London a very wealthy man, and the example below clearly demonstrates how this could be achieved.

This is a breakdown of the moneys for the first Boston talk:

Takings: Ticket Sales	$1,000
Minus: Business expenses:	$144.52
Carte Personal Expenses	$89.15
Profit	**$846.33**

The $846.33 was then split 50/50 as per the contract, giving both sides $423.16. There are many historical inflation sites to check to see what $423.16 is worth in today's economy. In 1882, $423.16 value in sterling at the time would have been £84 and 10 shillings. For the sake of ease, £85 in 1882 is the equivalent of £5,625.00 today. This a respectable sum, especially for a relatively unknown recent graduate. Bear in mind that was just the money from one of the talks on the tour. Of course not all of his talks sold out, not all venues were that big, but there was great potential for this tour to have set Wilde up financially for the foreseeable future. Oscar, however, was enjoying life on the road. Many of his expenses he would have argued were to keep up the illusion of Aestheticism and the aesthetic life style which, of course, included enjoying life's little luxuries. These little luxuries to make living on the road more comfortable included having full suites of rooms in the best hotels, travelling first class and eating at the best establishments.

Alongside these less than frugal options, Wilde managed to run up substantial private expenses. These personal expenses included wine, cigarettes, carriages, messages, newspapers, stamps, books and gloves. These ate in to Oscar's half of the profits quite significantly. His bad financial habits from his student days had clearly not improved, indeed they seem to have grown worse.

As his speaking tour continued Wilde decided to refresh and improve his personal aesthetic style. He wanted to maintain the image he had created with the portrait photographer Saroni at the beginning of the tour. This, of course, meant that he required more items for his wardrobe and subsequently ordered '2 velvet coats – tight fitting but with large flowered sleeves, [and] ruffs of cambric from the collar'. (Strugis, *Oscar,* p.234)

As well as evolving and tweaking his personal style Wilde decided to keep tinkering and updating his talk. It soon evolved to be renamed 'Decorative Arts' rather than 'The English Renaissance', and he drew more inspiration and included more about John Ruskin, William Morris, and the Dantes.

In February, the tour of America moved away from the east coast towards the Midwest. On his way towards Chicago, Oscar made a quick visit to Niagara Falls:

> It was not till I stood underneath the falls at Table Rock that I realised the majestic splendour and strength of the physical forces of nature here ... I thought of what Leonardo da Vinci said once 'the two most beautiful things in the world area woman's smile and the motion of water'.
>
> *The Buffalo Express,*
> 9 February 1882

He was somewhat less impressed with the protective outfit to keep him dry when he was on his tour of the falls as he wore an 'ugly' yellow oilskin.

The next few stops on his tour were Hartford in Connecticut on 2 February, Brooklyn in New York City on 3 February, then the following cities in New York State: Utica on 6 February, Rochester on 7 February, and Buffalo on 8 February. Buffalo was Oscar's last performance of the English Renaissance lecture.

After several days' rest, Wilde wrote to Colonel Morse from Chicago requesting the following of his tour management:

12 February 1882   Grand Pacific Hotel, Chicago

Dear Colonel Morse

I hope you will arrange some more matinées: *to lecture does not tire me.* I would sooner lecture five or six times a week and travel only three or four hours a day than lecture three times and travel 10 hours. I do not think I should ever lecture less than four times and these matinées are a great hit. Let me know what we do after Cincinnati – is it Canada? I am ready to lecture till the last week of April – 25 April say.

Yours truly,
Oscar Wilde

The request detailed in the letter shows an insight into trademark Oscar Wilde logic: work and travel as little as possible for maximum profit. It is also interesting that at this point of the tour he still expected to be en route back to Europe and the Parisian season in late April 1882.

Wilde found he got a warmer welcome from the people of Chicago than from their press. The locals were eager to hear him talk, as well as seem him in person – a living personification of Aestheticism. There were 2,500 people who came and attended his talk on 13 February, at the Central Music Hall, Chicago. It was Wilde's biggest audience yet and his new and improved lecture was mainly a hit with the locals. He did upset a few in the audience as he was particularly rude about the city's iconic water tower, calling it a 'castellated monstrosity with pepper boxes stuck all over it'. (*The Chicago Tribune*, 14 February 1882) and the local press were less than pleased at this slur at their iconic landmark. This did not put off the locals as Oscar would return to the city to lecture again on 11 March. Oscar made the Grand Pacific Hotel his base for the next few weeks as Colonel Morse accommodated Wilde's request to travel less and lecture more.

The next stops on his mid-west tour took in the towns and cities of Detroit, Cleveland, Louisville, Indianapolis, Cincinnati, St Louis and Springfield. On this leg of his lecturing tour Oscar had particular success in the cities of Cincinnati and St Louis. One of the biggest attractions for him in Cincinnati was city's cooperative craft pottery. This pottery's whole ethos was very much in line with the ideals and spirit of the Arts & Craft Movement that Wilde championed and loved. He was able to take a tour around the pottery and really enjoyed the experience. Wilde was taken with the city so much that he charmed his audience at the Grand Opera House when he exclaimed: 'I cannot express the delight it gives me that I stopped in your city and see the love you have for the beautiful art of decoration.' (*Cincinnati Gazette* 24 February 1882)

In a similar fashion Oscar loved the fact that St Louis had a distinguished school and museum of fine arts. But it was while in Louisville, Kentucky, that Wilde had his most exciting experience yet. After his talk on 21 February one Mrs Emma Speed, niece to the poet John Keats, approached Wilde. (The venue for this talk would have raised a smile for Wilde as it was in one of the city's masonic temples.) Mrs Speed was thrilled and delighted at Wilde's mention of her uncle in his speech and invited him to her home to see some of the items she had in relation to her uncle.

The next day, 22 February, Oscar took Mrs Speed up on her offer and paid her a visit. Oscar was able to look at letters from John Keats to her father, George Keats; hold pieces of manuscripts in his hand, and look at Keats's personal copy of Dante's *Divine Comedy*, with his handwritten notes in the margins. The pair must have gotten along very well as Emma Speed would later send Oscar the original manuscript for Keats's sonnet 'Blue!' Tis the life of Heaven, the domain'. The joy this gift gave Oscar is evident in his letter of thanks in March 1882:

21 March 1882   [Omaha, Nebraska]

What you have given me is more golden than gold, more precious than any treasure this great country could yield me … it is a sonnet I have loved always.

He continues:

> I am half enamoured of the paper that touched his hand and the ink that did his bidding … since my boyhood I have loved none better than your kinsman.

He then signs off in adoring Wilde style:

> in my heaven he walks eternally with Shakespeare and the Greeks … again I thank you for this memory of the man I love and thank you for the sweet and gracious words in which you gave it to me.

Wilde arrived back in Chicago on the last day of February. By the end of his second month in the United States, Wilde had found his rhythm as a lecturer. He had perfected and tweaked the talk he was giving and had found an agreeable way to balance talking, travelling and playing tourist. This would not last, however, as the pace and audience type were about to change. This return to the windy city was only brief.

The next part of his tour took him to Dubuque in Iowa; Rockford and Aurora in Illinois; Racine and Milwaukee in Wisconsin; Joliet, Jacksonville, Decatur, Peoria and Bloomington in Illinois, and back to Chicago. Unlike the first part of the circuit, these towns and cities were smaller and the audiences harder to lure. This was something of a reality check for Oscar. He had gone from audiences ranging from 1,000–2,500 and sold-out venues, to fewer than a hundred people in some cases. In Joliet only fifty-two individuals came to hear him talk.

It was reported in the *Chicago Tribune* on 7 March 1882, that when giving his talk to Racine he broke down, 'Midst his lecture saying he was exhausted and could not read his lines'. To add insult to injury, many of these smaller venues barely broke even – Joliet was actually a financial loss. Thankfully, this less than positive leg of his tour concluded in Chicago on 11 March.

Oscar had a few days to recuperate before heading to Minneapolis, Minnesota; Sioux City, Iowa and Omaha, Nebraska. These dates were certainly more positive than his previous few events. It was St Patrick's day (17 March) during his stay in Saint Paul, Minnesota. He was invited to attended an event for the feast day and ended up giving an impromptu speech on the 'Irish Question' and his thoughts on home rule. His politics towards his homeland were reflective of his politically active mother, who was known fondly within the Irish community of Saint Paul – who charmingly referred to Oscar as 'Speranza's gifted son'.

After his speaking engagement in Omaha, Oscar travelled further towards the south west of the northern American continent. Carte and Morse delegated this part of the tour to a different promotor by the name of Charles E. Lock. The terms and conditions with this new promotor were far less favourable than the terms with Carte and Morse. For fifteen lectures spread over three weeks in three states: Utah, California and Colorado, Wilde was given a set fee of $3,000. With Carte and Morse, profits were split 50/50. Although Carte and Morse's terms were higher risk, the potential for higher rewards was bigger too. Even so, $3,000 was no small sum in 1882.

In the 1880s the fastest way to travel from the mid-west to the south-western states was by train. This time is often described as the gilded age of rail travel in the US. However, it was still far from comfortable even when travelling First Class as Wilde naturally preferred to do. Oscar's journey took four days, with many stops and at a slow pace. Despite the length of the journey there was no catering on board, so Wilde would need to leave the train to take his meals at station restaurants. The tedious and uncomfortable journey would be worth the temporary discomfort when he finally arrived in San Francisco Bay.

The arrangement was very similar in San Francisco as it had been in Chicago. Oscar made San Francisco his central base from which he would travel to events around the city including: Oakland, San Jose, Sacramento and the sunset city itself, San Francisco. The reception that Wilde received in this part of the country was primarily positive and the people and warm climate would make it one of Oscar's favourite parts of his American adventure.

The first venue of these talks was held in Platts Hall in San Francisco on 27 March where the hosts had befittingly embellished the stage with a legion of fresh flowers in honour of their Aesthetic speaker. The venue would host four of the talks in this part of the tour. The fourth speech, held on 5 April, was special as it had been expressly sought and organised by the cultured elite of the city. For this extra talk, Wilde changed the topic to 'Irish Poets and Poetry of the nineteenth century'. Most of this new speech was based upon, and subsequently an improved version of, his impromptu speech given at Saint Paul on St Patrick's day. The subject also allowed him to include his mother's poetry as part of the lecture. This new talk was highly praised by the local press, especially the *San Francisco Chronicle*.

From sunny southern California Wilde resumed his partnership with Carte and Morse. The tour headed back east again. The stops on this part of the tour brought him to speak at Salt Lake City, Denver and Leadville. In correspondence dated 17 April 1882, from Nebraska, Wilde was less than complimentary about the audience in Salt Lake City. He says: 'I have lectured to the Mormons ... and they are very very ugly. The president, a nice old man sat with five wives in the stage box.' (Oscar Wilde, Kansas City, to Mrs Bernard Beere.)

This journey also took him to the heights of the Rocky Mountains thousands of feet above sea level. In the same letter Wilde describes the journey up the Rockies as: 'I have also lectured at Leadville, the great Mining city in the Rocky Mountains. We took a whole day to get up to it on a narrow-gauge railway 14,000 feet in height.' (Oscar Wilde, Kansas City, to Mrs Bernard Beere, 17 April 1882)

Wilde faced an unusual crowd on 12 April at Tabor Grand Opera House. His usual audiences were made up of cultured, the well educated – including students – wealthier and often predominantly married women. There for his audience at Tabour Opera house was a big change as it was made up of the town's miners. Goodness knows what these rough, hard-working nineteenth-century miners made of the flamboyant, long-haired velvet-bedecked speaker talking to them about interior designs and Aestheticism.

While in Denver, Oscar was given a tour and the opportunity to speak to the miners under ground. In order to head below the ground Wilde had to don a rubber suit and be lowered into the mine shaft by rope and a metal bucket. If Wilde had not been a fan of the mode of transport to the mine, this was quickly forgotten due to the warm welcome from the miners. These dirt covered men each had a bottle of whisky and by all accounts Wilde and his new friends enjoyed several hours of drinking and banter. When Wilde left, the miners had been impressed at his ability to hold drink.

Also while in Denver, Wilde was show the delights of the town's bars and was particularly taken by one sign hung in Bar Wyyman's Salon that read: 'Please do not shoot the pianist. He is doing his best.'

Like Charles Dickens before him, Wilde also took the opportunity to tour a US prison when offered a tour in Lincoln, Nebraska. The visit affected Wilde enough for him to describe it in detail to Helena Sickert, sister to the artist Walter Sickert, in a letter dated 25 April 1882 from Freemont, Nebraska.

> Poor sad types of humanity in hideous striped dresses making bricks in the sun, and all mean-looking, which consoled me, for I should hate to see a criminal with a noble face. little whitewashed cells, so tragically tidy, but in one I found a translation of Dante and Shelley. Strange and beautiful it seems to me that the sorrow of a Florentine in Exile should hundreds of years afterwards, lighten the sorrow of some common prisoner in a modern gaol.

There is a poignancy to these words written in 1882, as he himself was sentenced to hard labour, had to wear a prison uniform and found comfort when reading Dante in his cell at Reading Gaol. It could be argued that he would become the noble-faced prisoner among his fellow prisoners.

Amid his American journeys and lectures Oscar had not given up hope on his ambition to get his play *Vera* into production and onto the Broadway stage. D'Oyly Carte had initially taken great interest in *Vera* and the pair of them had even discussed terms and conditions. They had hoped that Canadian actress Clara Morris would take the leading lady role. Morris had been a somewhat successful stage actress in the 1870s, but had a reputation as difficult and flaky. Even after meeting Oscar and Carte, she decided to take a part in *Far From The Madding Crowd* instead of *Vera* for that theatre season. By the time she had confirmed she was not interested it was far too late to find a new actress, rehearse, and get the production onto the Broadway stage for spring/summer 1882. This was a big disappointment for Oscar, as well as a missed opportunity for D'Oyly Carte.

By May 1882, after five very busy non-stop months on the road touring and lecturing, Wilde arrived back in New York. Having failed to get *Vera* on to the stage, and initially expecting his tour to end there, Oscar instead decided to continue touring with the help of Carte and Morse as they had received requests that he revisit Philadelphia, New York, Boston and Cincinnati. Wilde was also eager to visit Canada. So that was how Oscar decided to miss the salon season of Paris in 1882 and spend more time in North America. By 10 May, he had returned to Philadelphia and while in the city took the opportunity to visit fellow poet Walt Whitman for a second time.

Whitman's sexuality is one of greatest debates among his researchers. He, unlike Wilde later on, was a very discreet and private individual, so there is little to no evidence confirming his sexuality one way or another. His researchers have had to examine the tone and language of his poems and look at some of his well-known friendships with various men. It is generally agreed that Whitman was homosexual. Later in life, while speaking with the early gay rights campaigner, George Cecil Ives in 1892, Wilde is reported to have said to him he had kissed Walt Whitman on the lips. Although there is no indication that Oscar had realised that he was homosexual at this time, the embrace and kiss with Whitman when he was parting from him seems to have left a mark on his memory.

In mid-May, Oscar finally made his way to Canada. The cities that he lectured in were: Montreal, Ottowa, Quebec City, Kingston, Bellville, Toronto, Woodstock and two dates in Hamilton. Given the sheer size of Canada this was an impressive achievement when travelling by train in the nineteenth century. By this point in the tour the nerves and teething problems of the early lectures had gone and Oscar had found his public speaking confidence. The reception of both the people and press of Canada was predominantly positive. He would return to the US on 2 June and give another talk in Boston before taking a well-earned nine day break using New York as his base. This break was needed as Oscar was about to undertake the most gruelling and taxing part of this tour yet; he was going to start touring the southern states of North America.

For the rest of June and most of July, Wilde took his lecture to the following cities: Memphis and Vicksburg in Mississippi; New Orleans, Louisiana; Galveston, San Antonio and Houston in Texas; back to New Orleans, then Mobile and Montgomery in Alabama; Columbus, Macon, Atlanta, Savannah and Augusta in Georgia; Charleston, South Carolina; Wilmington, North Carolina; Norfolk, and then Richmond in Virginia on 11 July 1882. These dates took Wilde to several southern states during the height of the southern summer. This would not have been a comfortable experience in nineteenth-century America. The constant train travel was starting to wear thin with Wilde, who resented train timetables ruling his life.

During this leg of the tour, Oscar was still accompanied by his African American Valet Traquair. During his travels in the southern former Confederate states of the US, Wilde was struck by the level of racial prejudice that was still present after the civil war in these states. Sadly, Wilde and Traquair were not immune to these unjust and cruel prejudices while they were travelling these states.

It was reported in in the *New York Times* on 9 July 1882, under the headline of 'Oscar Wilde and his Negro Valet', that while travelling between the Georgian cities of Atlanta and Savannah, Wilde attempted to take Traquair into the first-class sleeper car to tend him. Even though Traquair had been bought a ticket for this car, the staff from the railroad company tried to stop him boarding the carriage. Wilde was outraged and said that he had a ticket and he was not going to change the arrangement. Thankfully, a black rail porter discreetly spoke to both Wilde and Traquair and explained that if the locals saw a person of colour travelling in these carriages there was an extremely high risk that Traquair would be lynched. It was then that alternative arrangements were made for the valet. Wilde's defence and outrage towards the prejudice could have led to serious danger, both to himself and his valet. It is reassuring, however, that he was angered by the situation.

Wilde was starting to get weary of life on the road and this is clear in a letter to Colonel Morse dated late June 1882:

> Dear Colonel Morse
> It is very annoying to me to find that my Southern tour extends far beyond the three weeks you spoke of. It is now three weeks since I left New York and I am informed I have two weeks more. Five weeks for 16 lectures is quite ridiculous.

The tour of the south finally ended and Oscar arrived back in New York in the middle of July 1882. After giving a talk in Newport, Rhode Island, on 15 July, he was free of obligations until 2 August. During this period, Wilde visited his promotors' office and met up with Colonel Morse.

At this meeting they went through the financial figures for the tour to date. These figures are according to the data given in Matthew Sturgis's biography of Wilde:

The Total Receipts	$21,946.56
Minus Tour Costs (Travel, accommodation, promotional expenses etc)	$9,579.42
The net profit left to be split 50/50 as per the terms & conditions	$12,367.14
This gave Carte & co and Wilde (each)	$6,183.57

This is an extraordinary sum, however this was the amount including moneys already paid, and before Oscar's personal expenses were deducted. By this point in the tour, Oscar had accumulated a staggering $2,217.68 of costs made up of things such as tobacco, wine, newspapers, stamps telegrams, carriages and laundry costs. He had also already received $1,169.65 of his money from his share of the profits. This left him with $3,344.07 owed. When this figure is entered into historical financial calculators to work out how much that is in today's money, it generates the respectable sum profit of £44,000 today. Not bad for just over half a year's work.

While at this meeting, they also discussed the next part of Oscar's tour. There was still demand for him but Oscar was less keen to continue touring at the same fast pace. He wanted to have some down time. In the end they agreed to a further twenty lectures spread out over a six-week period, with plenty of time between lectures for Oscar to explore and relax.

These relaxed summer lectures started on 15 July in Newport and Rhode Island, before restarting again in Babylon New York on 2 August. Five days later Wilde once again took to the stage to talk at Narragansett Pier, New York. From the 9 until 19 August, Oscar was based in Catskill New York, but ventured to Long Beach on 16 August to speak to the locals. Next up was a short stay in New Jersey Shore that lasted from 21 until 26 August. He had a nice break until restarting the tour on 2 September and that first September date was in Saratoga Springs New York.

During the end of July and early August Oscar took one Mrs Julia Ward Howe up on her invitation for him to stay with her. In a letter dated 6 July 1882, he wrote to Mrs Howe about the arrangement of his visit in typical extravagant Wilde way:

My dear Mrs Howe
My present plan is to arrive in New York from Richmond on Wednesday evening and staying, if you will have me, till Saturday. I have an enormous trunk and a valet but they need not bother you. I can send them to the hotel.

He continues in fine form:

> But I can't travel without Balzac and Gautier, and they
> take up so much room: and as long as I can enjoy talking
> nonsense to flowers and children I am not afraid of the
> deprived luxury of a hat-box.

Other notable highlights from Wilde's leisure time between talks
included swimming at Long Beach, sipping champagne and attending
the opening meeting of the Newport Polo season. He was also said to
have been found entertaining small children at his hotel in Babylon, by
inventing fairytales for their amusement; this was something he greatly
enjoyed doing for his own sons, Cyril and Vyvyan. He also was given
the opportunity to hobnob with a former President, Ulysses S. Grant.

For the rest of September Oscar found himself moving around the
beautiful states of New England. His next engagement would be on
25 September in Providence, Rhode Island, where he gave his now
well-rehearsed speech at Law's Grand Opera House. The pace started
to resume to a pre-summer rhythm as the following day, 26 September,
he spoke to the people of Salem, Massachusetts, and then the people
of Lynn, Massachusetts, on 27 and 28 September. Wilde then found
himself back in Rhode Island in the town of Pawtucket for the 29th,
North Attleborough Massachusetts on the 30th, before concluding this
part of the tour on 3 October in Bangor, Maine.

Even during this more relaxed period during the summer lecturing
tour, Wilde was still attempting to get *Vera* onto the New York stage.
He would make contact with Mary Anderson an influential American
actress in the vain hope that she would help him. During September
alone Oscar wrote three letters to her. The tone of his last letter dated
September 1882 starts to sound unctuous, as he seeks her help:

> If you desire, as I feel that you at any rate do, to create an
> era in the history of American dramatic art, and to take your
> assured rank among the great artist of our time, here is the

opportunity: and remember we live in an age when without art there is really no true success, *financially* or otherwise.

The last lecture Oscar gave in North America was on 13 October 1882 at St John, New Brunswick. In all, Oscar Wilde had given 140 lectures in 130 locations, and travelled over 15,000 miles in an era without air travel. During his time in North America and Canada, he had made the philosophy of Aestheticism a recognisable and understood term, become a household name and a recognisable public figure. The 10½ month tour had been nothing less than a triumphant success for the Dublin-born poet and Classicist, newly graduated from Oxford University. The star of Mr Oscar Fingal O'Flahertie Wills Wilde was beginning to ascend.

THE THEATRE AND THE
BEAUTIFUL PEOPLE

'I regard the theatre as the greatest of all art forms.'
Oscar Wilde

While the lecture tour had come to an end in north America and Canada, Oscar decided he wanted to stay on in the land of opportunities a little while longer.

Despite his best efforts to have a volume of his mother's poetry published in the US, nothing came of it. At the same time, his priority was to get *Vera* onto the Broadway stage. With help from Colonel Morse, the first step was to get a tweaked copy of the play copyrighted on that side of the Atlantic. Once this was achieved the pair then sent out this new copyrighted manuscript to anyone whom Morse thought might be interested in it or could help them. Among those who were sent a copy of the new version of *Vera* were theatre managers and potential leading actresses.

From one of those mailouts, Wilde made the acquaintance of Steele MacKaye; a jack-of-all-theatrical-trades. He was a playwright, producer, acting teacher, stage manager, theatre manager, inventor and a fellow aesthete. Two of the many inventions created by MacKaye were the familiar flip-down chairs all theatres and cinemas around the globe use today, as well as the 'nebulator' – a machine that was able to create realistic artificial clouds on stage – surprisingly modern for the nineteenth century.

Several meetings between MacKaye and Wilde took place at one of their favourite locations in New York, The Lamb Club – which had a suitably bohemian and aesthetic decor and atmosphere. As well as talking about *Vera* Oscar also sounded out MacKaye's views about a new idea he was working on, a play set in Renaissance Italy. Wilde also resumed his correspondence with the influential Mary Anderson, on the topic of both these projects. The play set in Renaissance Italy was titled *The Duchess of Padua*, and was yet to be written. Negotiations with Mary regarding the terms, conditions and costs were ongoing. Oscar would have completed a script for *The Duchess of Padua*, by the end of March, 1883. All these new plans for the theatre meant that any prospect of Oscar taking his lecturing tour to the Antipodes, was put on hold indefinitely.

With regards to *Vera*, MacKaye liked the play but felt that it still required refining. This did not stop Oscar and himself looking for potential leading ladies to take the main role. The most enthusiastic of the actresses that they contacted was 29-year-old Marie Prescott.

In late October 1882, Oscar had a taste of home come to New York, as his friend Lillie Langtry arrived to make her US acting debut. She was starting on Broadway before touring the rest of the nation. Lillie Langtry was born on the island of Jersey on 13 October 1853 and was given the name Emilie Charlotte Le Breton. She married in 1874 to Edward Langtry, whose surname became part of her stage name throughout her career, despite divorcing Langtry in 1897. The couple remained on Jersey until 1876 when, aged 23, they relocated to London. Once in the English capital, she was able to integrate into the literary, middle upper-class circles of society with ease. She became a leading model and muse for the artists of the Aesthetic Movement, and it was through these connections that she got to know Oscar Wilde. In 1881 she made her London acting debut before heading over to America at the end of the following year.

Oscar was happy to become Lillie's guide to New York City, particularly during her first few weeks in the Big Apple. Wilde would prove to be invaluable when misfortune befell Langtry. The Abbey Park Theatre, situated in the Flatiron District of Manhattan, went up in flames the night before Langtry was to make her American debut with the play

An Unequal Match. The disaster is mentioned in a letter written by Wilde on 31 October 1882: 'Poor Mrs Langtry is dreadfully upset by the catastrophe; she had only left the theatre a few hours.' (*Complete Letters of Oscar Wilde* p.188) Thankfully only a small delay was caused by the fire and An Unequal Match found a new venue at the nearby Wallack's Theatre and Langtry made her US debut on 6 November 1882. Oscar did manage to pick up a few small freelance writing commissions during the last few weeks in New York, one of which was from the *New York World* to write about Langtry's performance from an aesthetic viewpoint.

In early December Langtry left New York to take the production on tour. Not long afterwards Oscar fell ill with what he claimed to be Malaria. There is a chance that he contracted the parasitic infection while in the southern states during the heat of the summer. Some of those southern states can have a tropical climate and subsequently attract the disease-carrying mosquitoes. Whatever the illness was, this combined with Langtry departing on her own US adventure, Oscar realised it was now time to go back home. He booked a birth on SS *Bothnia*, and left New York on 27 December 1882 for Liverpool, England.

By all accounts the return journey to Liverpool was far rougher than Wilde's outward-bound voyage the year before. Despite the uncomfortable journey, Oscar arrived back in Liverpool on 6 January 1883, a year to the day since he stepped foot on American soil. Wilde's mother was pleased to have her youngest son back and Oscar stayed with his mother in London, while he decided what to do next. Among the friends with whom Wilde became reacquainted during his brief sojourn back in London was the American artist James Abbot McNeill Whistler, whom Oscar referred to as Jimmy. Wilde mentions 'Jimmy' in a letter dated 31 January 1883 to the American sculptor, Waldo Story:

> I saw a great deal of Jimmy in London *en passant.* He has just finished a second series of Venice Etchings – such water-painting as the gods never beheld. His exhibition opens in a fortnight in a yellow and white room ... with a catalogue which is amazing.

During this period back in London, Oscar sensibly sought out advice from a financial advisor, one Edwin Levy, to help him manage what was left of his profits from the US tour. Unfortunately in that last quarter of 1882, when he was living in New York and not lecturing, Oscar spent a fair chunk of the profits he had made from the previous nine months. He also had to pay for his accommodation during this period, whereas previously it had been paid for him. This, and his overly generous nature in regards to money, meant he had arrived back to the UK a lot less well off than both he and his creditors expected. Although his finances were not in the best state, there was still enough profit left to enable him to pay for a jaunt across the channel to spend some time in the city of love and lights, Paris.

By the end of January 1883 Oscar had arrived in Paris. He intended this time to be used in order to work on refining *Vera* and completing the script for *The Duchess of Padua*. Like many artists before and after him, Wilde lodged on the artistic left bank of the River Seine. He chose to stay at the Hôtel Voltaire, which was positioned opposite the Musée Louvre. The air of Paris seems to have had a positive effect on Wilde's ability to write, as the words for *The Duchess of Padua* seemed to flow; so much so that Oscar was able to complete and deliver the play two weeks ahead of his deadline on 15 March 1883. During this period, Wilde was introduced to Èmile Zola. '*Je vous remercie bien de votre courtoise, et de votre introduction à M. Zola, de laquelle je ne manquerai pas de me profiter*' ('I thank you very much for your courtesy, and for your introduction to Mr Zola, from which I will not fail to benefit.' (*Complete Letters of Oscar Wilde* p.207)

Next, Oscar turned his attention back to refining and fine tuning the script for *Vera*. Marie Prescott was still as rhapsodic towards the production and eventually Wilde and Prescott were able to negotiate a good deal. Prescott wanted full control over the practicalities such as casting and costumery, as well as being completely happy with the final script. Financially, Wilde got a generous deal, he would get $1,000 up front and then $50 per performance – at seven performances a week sometimes eight (if there is an extra matinée added) that is $350–$400 dollars a week passive income for the run of the production.

Marie Prescott was born in the US state of Kentucky, in 1850. At age 27, in 1877, she made her stage debut in Cincinnati in a production of Shakespeare's *Macbeth* as the female lead, *Lady Macbeth*. Through her negotiations with Wilde, Prescott bought the rights to *Vera* and opened the play for the first time on 20 August 1883. The play was not well received by the New York press and the run only lasted a week. Prescott would work as an actress and producer for a further ten years, eventually retiring from the stage in spring of 1893. She died four months later at the age of 43.

Prior to his trip in 1883, Oscar had been a frequent visitor to Paris. As a child and student he had acquired a good level of conversational French. During his few months in the city in early 1883, his fluency continued to improve to the point that he felt comfortable writing poetry in the French language. He even took to writing correspondences to his mother in French.

It was also during this sojourn in Paris that Oscar took the time to recreate and change his personal style. While he was writing *The Duchess of Padua*, he decided to mimic one of his French literary heroes, Honoré de Balzac, by wearing a white dressing gown known as a *burnous*. Balzac was known for wearing one as he worked. Oscar also changed up his outdoor fashion, swapping his breeches, for tight-fitting long trousers and shirt. To go with this, he cut his longer hair and had what was left of his hair artificially curled. It is thought that he found inspiration from a bust of the notorious Roman Emperor, Nero in the Musée Louvre. To finish this new and unique new look, he accessorised with an ivory walking cane, that would remain part of his style long after he left Paris.

Once Oscar had completed the script for *The Duchess of Padua*, he was able to enjoy the social delights on offer in the city. Due to his friendship with 'Jimmy' Whistler, Oscar was able to integrate with the Impressionist artists who were thriving in Paris at this time.

It was around this period and once back in London, that Oscar started to pay court to the future to Constance Wilde. His social circle and peers comprised a veritable collection of up-and-coming socialites and artistic and literary persons. As well as knowing Lillie Langtry, Wilde was also friendly with another of the leading actresses of the Victorian era, Ellen Terry.

Born Alice Ellen Terry on 27 February 1846, there was little doubt as to what her future would hold, for she had been born into a family of thespians and began acting in her childhood. By 16 she had already married to George Fredrick Watts thirty years her senior at 46 years old. Unsurprisingly, the marriage lasted barely a year – although it would take until 1877 before they were legally divorced. Not long after leaving Watts she started a relationship with Edward William Godwin, with whom she had two children. For the majority of the period of this relationship, Terry did not perform on the stage, only returning to performing in 1874, a year before the relationship failed. Her stage comeback was a great success and she became associated with playing leading female roles in Shakespearian plays. Wilde first saw Terry perform in December 1878, in a play called *New Men and Old Acres*. This was the start of Wilde's frequent visits to watch Ellen perform. He was often so moved by her performances that he would compose sonnets to her and even sent her several. In turn Terry was greatly flattered by this younger man's written devotion to her, in the form of beautiful lines of poetry.

Wilde approached Terry in the hope that she would take on the lead role *Vera*, but she politely turned down his offer. Their respect and friendship was very much mutual and he gave her the nickname of 'Our Lady of the Lyceum', as she was part of the Lyceum theatres company of actors. Wilde and Terry were mutual friends of Lilly Langtry and the two actresses were supportive of each other's work and careers. In 1888 Wilde sent Terry a copy of his book of short fairytales, *The Happy Prince and Other Tales*, and Terry was complimentary in her return. When Oscar's world fell apart in 1895, Ms Terry remained loyal to him, sending a bouquet of Violets which signified her faithfulness to her friend, as well as a horseshoe for good luck. She also reached out to offer support to Constance during this period. The last time that Terry saw her friend was in 1900, when she was visiting Paris with a mutual friend Amy Lowther. They had been saddened and shocked at how he appeared, and at his impoverished state. However, the three had a meal together where Wilde, despite his downturn in fortune, was as witty and jovial as his former self. Terry would outlive Wilde by twenty-eight years, dying in 1928 having achieved a highly successful acting career spanning seven decades.

As mentioned earlier, on 29 May 1884, Oscar Wilde married Constance Lloyd in St James's Church, Paddington, London. The pair honeymooned in Paris, then spent the rest of the year settling into married life and curating their home on Tite Street. They would be close to their circle of literary and artistic friends. With marriage, came the birth of Oscar's two sons, Cyril in 1885, followed by Vyvyan in 1886. It was not long after the birth of Vyvyan, that Oscar became acquainted with Robbie Ross and he started to explore his homosexuality (more of this later).

With new responsibilities, Oscar needed to find a stable income to support his family and aesthetic lifestyle. Although the couple had an income from Constance's allowance, Oscar wanted to contribute too. Between 1886 and 1889 he became the editor of the Victorian women's journal *The Lady's World*. It was during his time at the helm that the magazine changed its name from *The Lady's World* to *The Woman's World*, and changed the content of the publication to be more about what Victorian women felt and thought, rather than just social tittle-tattle and fashion. The initial excitement of a new venture soon wore off for Wilde, who started to appear in the office less and less often. He would rather be writing his own plays and poetry than commissioning writers and editing other writers' work for a magazine aimed at women.

During his time at *The Woman's World*, Wilde was working on his only full novel, *The Picture of Dorian Gray*. This would be published in a short form by US Publication *Lippincott's Monthly Magazine*, in July 1890, and would subsequently be published in its full-length format in April 1891.

During its serialisation in *Lippincott's Monthly Magazine*, there was great concern over the content and themes of *The Picture of Dorian Gray*. The version that was published in the magazine had been edited by the publication, taking about 500 words out of the story without Oscar's knowledge. One of the main concerns was that the deleted passages insinuated, if not directly implied, homosexual feelings and desires between some of the characters. Even with these changes made by *Lippincott's Monthly Magazine*, WH Smiths withdrew all copies of the magazine from its retailers, which were predominantly located in railways stations during the 1890s.

In the subsequent publication of the full novel, Wilde choose to retain these edits, and to make further changes to the text himself. He would create chapters 3, 5 and 15–18 as new chapters. He then adapted and changed one of the existing chapters by splitting it in two, expanding upon the two new chapters' texts. These would become chapters 19 and 20 in the final copy. He also added a preface to the novel. This improved, edited and expanded version of *The Picture of Dorian Gray*, would be published by Ward, Lock and Company in April, 1891, but not until Wilde was happy with the final edited copy. In June 1890, Wilde wrote to Ward, Lock and Company saying the following: 'Gentlemen, Kindly do not send out any more copies of Messrs Lippincott's puff of my book. It is really an insult to the critics. Also will you kindly let me know if I can have an interview with you on Thursday Morning at twelve o'clock.' (Complete Letters of Oscar Wilde p.433) Professional critics of the time were rather unfavourable towards the novel, indeed some of the worst claims by the critics were that it was 'vulgar', 'unclean', 'poisonous', and that it was a 'mawkish and nauseous story' that constantly hinted at 'disgusting sins and abominable crimes'.

With reviews such as this, the book caused a scandal, and with scandal came public demand. Although not ideal, Wilde had generated publicity for his work and was starting to become known. Wilde himself almost perfectly sums this up in one of his most famous quotations taken from the book itself, in Chapter 1: 'There is only one thing in life worse than being talked about and that is not being talked about.' *The Picture of Dorian Gray*, however, would be Oscar's only full novel. He decided to redirect his talents back to writing for the stage again; this time in the form of his play *Lady Windermere's Fan*, that would be a four act comedy.

To summarise, Lady Windermere is about to hold a ball for her birthday. She has grown suspicious about the behaviour of her husband, Lord Windermere, and assumes that he is having an affair. She, of course, confronts her husband, who proceeds to deny that he is being unfaithful. Much to Lady Windermere's shock, Lord Windermere invites Mrs Erlynne, the woman whom she believes him to be having an affair with, to her birthday ball, and naturally she becomes angry. Subsequently she decides to leave Lord Windermere, with the intention of having an affair herself. Mrs Erlynne goes after Lady Windermere to persuade her to return to her husband, and in the course of their exchange, Lady Windermere discovers that Mrs Erlynne is not her husband's lover, but is in fact her own mother, who had abandoned her twenty years previously. Some of Wilde's best-known quotations come from the play, a favourite being: 'We are all in the gutter, but some of us are looking at the stars,' spoken by Lord Darlington in Act 3. The play opened in London, on 20 February 1892, at St James's Theatre. In financial terms, the play was a success and generated an income of £7,000 in 1892–3 alone – a sum that would be the equivalent to between £600,000 – £800,000 today.

At the beginning of 1892, Wilde was approached by the company of actors at the Theatre Royal Haymarket, to write a new play. This play would become *A Woman of No Importance*. The majority of its writing took place during a holiday in Norfolk, during the summer of 1892. It is rather surprising that the play was finished, as the holiday and Wilde's writing time was constantly interrupted by the attention seeking of Bosie. The complete work was submitted to the Haymarket, in October 1892, and had its first performance at the theatre, on 19 April 1893. The play was well received and ran from mid-April until August of the same year. However, Wilde's next piece for the theatre was far more controversial and would create a scandal of its own – the play in question was *Salomé*.

Since 1737, right up until 1968 and the introduction of the Theatres Act, all plays planned to be performed in public had to be checked and given authorisation by the Lord Chamberlain. This was to ensure that decorum and public peace was maintained. Censorship in the theatre, was by no means new; prior to the law change in 1737, the task of approving entertainments was the responsibility of the Master of the Revels; a royal post of government created in 1347. Even the great works of William Shakespeare had to be submitted and checked ahead of a first performance, to ensure that there was nothing controversial, blasphemous, treasonous or excessively profane. So, Victorian playwrights, such as Oscar Wilde were obliged to have all their works checked prior to public performance.

As approval was seen as a certainty, rehearsals started prior to receiving the legal approval. In 1891, Wilde had started to rehearse *Salomé* for a run at the Royal Opera House in Covent Garden. The leading lady was none other than the renowned French actress, Sarah Bernhardt.

Sarah Bernhardt could easily be described as the first modern star of stage and later screen. She was born on 22 October 1844 in Paris with the name Sara Marie Henriette Rosine Bernard, to a Dutch Jewish high society courtesan mother, and an unknown father. Her exact paternal parentage is not known and she often used her maternal uncle's name as her father on official forms to avoid the embarrassment of illegitimacy. She would change her name for professional purposes adding the additional 'H' to her first and surname.

Bernhardt's stage career started in 1862, but it was a rough start and she was not an instant success. But with each new role she grew in confidence. He breakthrough would come in 1868 in an adaptation of the Alexandre Dumas novel *Kean*, in which she played the role of Anna Damby. During the Franco-German war 1870–1, when life in Paris came to a standstill, Bernhardt turned the Odéon Théâtre into a military hospital to care for injured French soldiers. She did not just organise this endeavour, but was also actively nursing and assisting in operations. By the time the conflict had ended, the Odéon hospital had cared for 150 injured French soldiers.

She resumed her acting career after the Paris Commune fell, in May 1871. By 1880 Sarah Bernhardt had put together her own independent acting company so that she no longer needed to be contracted to a specific theatre. This was an extraordinary achievement for an actress in the latter part of the nineteenth century. It was with this company of actors that Sarah made an international name for herself in Europe, the United Kingdom and the United States of America. Bernhardt debuted in New York was on 8 November 1880 on New York's Booth's Theatre stage with a performance of *Adrienne Lecouvreur*, a play about the eighteenth-century French actress of the same name, and it was a critical success. She returned to the United States a further eight times during the rest of her career, the last visit being in 1916, during the First World War. She also carried out subsequent tours that took her to Australia and South America.

Bernhardt did not just play female roles, she also undertook the lead role in *Hamlet* in both Paris and London. She also became one of the first actresses to work in film. Her silver screen debut was in 1900, in a film entitled *Le Duel d'Hamlet*. She liked the medium, but it would be a further nine years until she appeared in the cinema again in a film version of *La Tosca*, in 1909. It would be her role in the film adaptation of *La dame aux Camelias* in 1912, at the grand age of 68, that was both a popular and critical success. She went on to make a further eight films, the last, when she was 79, in 1923 entitled *La Voyante* (*The Fortune Teller*). The film was released posthumously in October 1924, as Sarah Bernhardt died on 26 March 1923. She would be buried in Paris's most prestigious cemetery, Pere Lachaise just like Wilde.

Rehearsals for *Salomé* came to an abrupt end when the Lord Chamberlain's office deemed the production blasphemous, due to the use of biblical characters. Anyone who has seen a production of the play even today may find some of the later scenes eye-opening, so to a conservative Victorian audience the play would have been nothing short of scandalous. Wilde eventually had *Salomé* published in France two years later in 1893; however, it would not be performed – even in Paris – for a further three years, in 1896, while Wilde was serving his sentence for gross indecency at Reading Gaol. It was a one-off performance on 11 February 1896, at the Théâtre de la Comedies-Parisienne – and it was not even the main performance, it was the second in a double bill. Wilde never saw this play performed. Eight months later *Salomé* was part of a

Wilde double bill with a translated version of *Lady Windermere's Fan* also in Paris, at the Nouveau-Théâtre. *Salomé* was then adapted into an opera by German Composer Richard Strauss and was performed in 1905 to an audience in Dresden in December of that year. It would be a further five years (ten after Wilde's death) before the play would be performed in London in 1910, having undergone heavy editing from the Chamberlain's office.

Wilde seems to have learnt his lesson and decided to be less controversial for his next two pieces of theatre, which are probably his most well known and loved – they would also be his last two; they were *An Ideal Husband* and *The Importance of Being Earnest*.

Initially, *An Ideal Husband* was turned down by the man who had commissioned, *A Woman of No Importance*, John Hare. He was the manager of the Royal Haymarket Theatre. Wilde was never one to give up, and he offered the play to Lewis Waller instead, who was just about to temporarily take over the running of the Haymarket as a favour for Hare.

The rehearsals started in December 1894 and *An ideal Husband* premiered at the Haymarket on 3 January 1895. Wilde generously gave Robbie Ross two tickets for the performance. The play would run for a total of 111 performances and its last night happened to be the same evening that Wilde was arrested for gross indecency. Despite Wilde's arrest the play was not shelved, it merely changed theatre, to the London Criterion, where the theatre prudently took Wilde's name off the billing and programmes. Given the scandal unfolding at the time, it is quite an achievement that the Criterion ran the play from the 13 to 27 April. The play itself was published during Wilde's lifetime, with a limited number of a thousand copies printed, in 1899.

While *An ideal Husband* was playing at the Haymarket, the last of Wilde's plays was preparing to be debuted on the London stage, and it is arguably his best-known play: *The Importance of Being Earnest*. Wilde had started work on *The Importance of Being Earnest* in 1894 while the Wilde family took their last family holiday together, in the southern coastal town of Worthing. It was not an easy writing experience, as during this holiday Wilde found his time being manipulated by the demanding Bosie. When the play was completed, he was able to find a theatre willing to put it on due to a fortunate set of circumstances.

The St James's Theatre was showing *Guy Domville* by Henry James in January 1895. Unfortunately for James, the play was a commercial washout and closed early. This allowed Wilde to fill the gap with *The Importance of Being Earnest*. It premiered on 14 February, and on that same evening the Marquess of Queensberry attempted to cause trouble with a bouquet of rotten cabbages at the stage door. Wilde had suffered harassment from Bosie's father for over eighteen months previous to the run up to opening night of the play. Wilde was alerted to the fact that the marquess had bought tickets for opening night, and on 13 February, requested that the theatre write to him. 'Dear Mr Shone, Lord Queensberry is at Carter's Hotel, Albemarle Street. Write to him from Mr Alexander that you regret to find that the seat given to him was already sold and return him his money. This will prevent trouble, I hope Yours truly, Oscar Wilde.'

Wilde wore a green carnation in his buttonhole to the premier, it was a discreet Victorian code shared among the gay community. The meaning of the green carnation was first brought to Wilde's attention during a trip to Paris with Bosie. Wilde made wearing a green carnation popular in London, and started to wear one in his buttonhole as early as 1892, when he donned one to the premier of *Lady Windermere's Fan*. Given that this is three years prior to his arrest, Wilde was by no means hiding his new-found awakening to anyone who knew the codes.

After Wilde's arrest, the St James's Theatre tried to continue with *The Importance of Being Earnest* by removing Wilde's names from billing and programmes. The play was able to reach eighty-six performances before it closed its first run. It also managed to get a very brief Broadway run at the Empire Theatre, New York, opening on 22 April 1895. Inevitably, as the details of Wilde's arrest travelled across the Atlantic, it only managed sixteen performances before closing.

This period of Oscar's life was the most successful of his promising career as a writer and playwright. In fact, as his trial was taking place,

A nineteenth-century sketch of poet and playwright Oscar Wilde.

MR. OSCAR WILDE.

Plaque in Rome's Protestant cemetery for John Keats.

The gravestone for English Romantic poet John Keates in Rome's Protestant cemetery visited by Wilde.

English Romantic poet Percy Shelley's grave n Rome's Protestant cemetery visited by Wilde.

Oscar Wilde's Signiture.

Oscar Wilde, photographed in New York, for use during his American tour in 1882.

Oscar Wilde photgraphed in New York, for use during his American tour in 1882.

Oscar Wilde while a student at Magdalen College Oxford.

Image of Oscar Wilde published in *Punch* magazine.

PUNCH'S FANCY PORTRAITS.—No. 37.

Oscar Wilde's grave monument in Cimetière du Père-Lachaise, Paris. Image taken by author.

Front view of Oscar Wilde's grave monument in Cimetière du Père-Lachaise, Paris. Image taken by author.

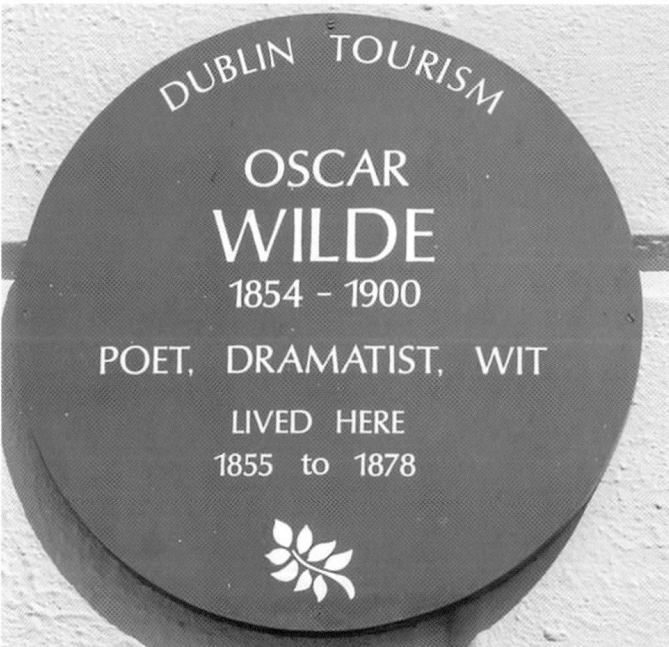

Dubin tourism plaque on the Wildes home in Merrion Square Dublin, Ireland.

The exterior of the hotel in Paris where Oscar Wilde died in 1900. Formerly Hôtel d'Alsace now called L'Hotel.

The front page of *Police News*, 4 May 1895.

Left: Monument to Oscar Wilde near Charing Cross, London. Created by Artist M. Hamlin. Image by author.

Below: Wilde's calling card with his new post-prison identity: Sebastian Melmoth.

Bottom: The calling card that the Marquis of Queensberry left at Wilde's club. (National Archives)

M͞ʳ SEBASTIAN MELMOTH

Berneval-sur-Mer, près Dieppe

Above: St James's Theatre pictured 1890.

Right: Picture of Oscar Wilde and his lover Lord Alfred Douglas. Known as "Bosie".

Image of Salomé from 1907 by Aubrey Beardsley.

Plaque commemorating when and where Wilde met with *Sherlock Holmes* author Arthur Conan Doyle.

A programme for Wilde's lecture in Boston, part of his 1882 US Tour.

Image of Oscar wearing a green carnation – a green carnation in the buttonhole was a code used among gay men during the Victorian era.

Above: Image of Wilde taken to publicise his US Tour in 1882.

Left: Poster advertising one of Wilde's Talks in the US.

Constance Wilde not long after her marriage to Oscar.

Oscar, Constance and their eldest son Cyril on holiday.

Left: Constance with her eldest son Cyril.

Below: Plaque depicting Oscar Wilde on the side of L'Hotels, Paris.

Vyvyan, Oscar's youngest son, with Oscar's grandson Merlin, 1954.

A younger Robbie Ross.

Robbie Ross in 1911. (Elliott & Fry)

The memorial statue of Oscar Wilde located in Merrion Square, Dublin.

two of his plays were being performed in London at the same time. He was surrounded by creative and artistic people, many of whom he considered friends, such as Lillie Langtry, Ellen Terry, James Whistler, Sarah Bernhardt, Arthur Conan Doyle and Bernard Shaw. Sadly, this period of success would abruptly change in the spring of 1895, when his private life became very public thanks to the legal trials with the Marquess of Queensberry. This turn of events would not just affect Wilde, professionally and financially, but also his reputation and the lives of his wife and children.

THE STATE OF MARRIAGE: CONSTANCE'S STORY

*'Marriage is the triumph of
imagination over intelligence.'*

Oscar Wilde

It is not possible to write a biography of Oscar Wilde without looking at one of the most important women in his life, his wife and the mother of his children, who was loyal friend to her end, Constance Lloyd. This chapter looks at her role in his life, but of course she appears throughout the book as well.

It is worth looking at Constance's parents to understand a little of how this extraordinary woman was brought up and became the woman Oscar married. Her mother's childhood city was Dublin, a connection Constance had to Wilde's home city. Constance's mother was Adelaide Barbara Atkinson and her childhood home was 1 Ely Place, in the grander Georgian area of the Irish capital. She also had an uncle, Charles Hare, who resided on Merrion Square, the same residential square as Oscar's parents, Lady and Dr Wilde.

At 19 years old, Ada, as she was known to her friends and family, married an English lawyer, Horace Lloyd who also happened to also be her cousin. Upon marrying, the couple moved to Horace's home city of London, where they started their married life in the smart neighbourhood of Marylebone. Constance Lloyd was their second child on 2 January 1858, in their London home in Marylebone, London. Constance's elder brother had been born two years previously on the 12 November 1856, and had been christened Otho.

Once Horace Lloyd, had begotten two children, he very quickly grew tired of traditional family and married life, and preferred to spend his time mixing with the Prince of Wales and his fraternity of cronies, in the atmosphere of London's many gentlemen's clubs and Freemason lodges.

To give some indication of the type of company Lloyd was keeping, the Prince of Wales at this time was Albert Edward, the eldest son of Queen Victoria and Prince Albert; he would go on to become King Edward VII. While he was waiting in the wings of his mother's long reign, Albert, who was known by his friends and family as Bertie, was something of a playboy, who openly enjoyed the freedom of having no occupation and access to lots of money – just like many British aristocrats of the period. The fathers of both Constance and Oscar were of the same ilk. This may go some way to explain the more tolerant view of infidelity within the marriage of Oscar and Constance marriage, and how Constance behaved towards her husband's infidelities. This in turn may explain Oscar's readiness to break his marriage vows to Constance through his liaisons and affairs with men.

Neither Ada nor Horace could have been described as nurturing parents; in fact, all sources describe them both as 'selfish', 'egotistical' and, in her mother's case, 'difficult' from as early as 19 years old. This gives us a fair indication of the main reason why Constance's father was constantly absent from the family home, during the early part of her life. Like Oscar, Constance had a less than conventional childhood, particularly given the social class she belonged to an era that they were both born into.

As her parents' marriage fell apart behind closed doors, Ada started to bring her children over to Dublin fairly frequently in order to be close to her family, particularly her mother. While on these visits the Lloyd children often visited their Uncle Charles and their cousins in Merrion Square, so it was entirely possible that Constance and Oscar knew of each other as children. Constance certainly would have known who the Wildes were, given the scandal of Dr Wilde and his court case, and because of the fashionable literary salons held by Lady Wilde.

Constance's ill health started in her childhood when she, like many Victorian children, contracted both chickenpox and then measles. In an era without vaccines for either childhood illness (the measles vaccine was introduced to the UK in 1968 and chickenpox vaccine as late as 1995). Constance was one of the lucky ones and survived both in a time when these childhood illnesses could be fatal. One of the biggest factors in her survival would have been her wealth and social status, which allowed access to fresh nutritious food, clean water and medical help, unlike many poor children of the time.

While it may not have been domestic happiness within the Lloyd family, they were fiscally mobile and were able to move to the more distinguished neighbourhood of Sussex Gardens in London. The two Lloyd children would both benefit from having a good education – even Constance. During this period the education of girls was limited to the basics, and training them to become good homemakers. Among her accomplishments she was able to play the piano, speak French and read Italian. Her level of education went on to allow her to be able to apply to, and be accepted by, UCL – one of the few colleges of the time that admitted female students. Even after they had completed their studies however, the few lucky women admitted by UCL were not awarded, or allowed to hold, degrees for all their hard work.

It is easy to see, therefore, why Oscar found Constance such an appealing companion. Unlike many of her peers, she was educated, articulate, and had opinions of her own. Both Oscar and Constance were also big supporters of the Dress Reform Movement.

The love story of Constance and Oscar started on 6 June 1881, at one of Speranza's literary get togethers in their Dublin Home in Merrion Square. Given the intelligent sparky nature of Constance, she would have stood out from her peers in a way that appealed to the intellectual and literary sensibilities of Oscar. One of the passions they shared was a love of the English poet, John Keats. The pair had hit it off so well that Oscar paid Constance a visit the following day imploring her to come to more of his mother's literary gatherings at Merrion Square.

As their friendship grew, Constance's family were not as impressed with Oscar as she was. Both his parents were 'notorious' for different reasons, and they regarded Oscar as garish and flashy and only using Constance for her wealth, rather than for nobler truer reasons.

Despite these reservations from her family, the friendship between Oscar and Constance inevitably turned into a courtship during the summer of 1883. The pair were constantly chaperoned by either Lady Wilde or Constance's brother Otho. During their courtship, Oscar undertook another speaking tour, this time in the UK and Ireland. It was somewhat less lucrative than his US tour had been but was still an income. It was also during this time that *Vera* finally opened on Broadway. He returned briefly to the US ahead of the opening, sailing on SS *Britannic*.

Sadly, *Vera* was not the hit show that all parties hoped for and only lasted twenty-eight days on the New York stage. However, he returned to London and continued his speaking tour around the UK and Ireland. By the end of 1883, Oscar had decided to cement his relationship with Constance and propose marriage to her. The opportunity came up when he was back in Dublin for part of his speaking tour in late 1883. Oscar's lectures in Dublin were scheduled for the 22 and 24 November 1883, and it just so happened that Constance was also back in the city visiting her family at the time. She attended both of Oscar's talks, and on 25 November she and Oscar went for tea after his second lecture. It was In the drawing room of her maternal grandmother, in 1 Ely Place, Dublin, that Oscar Wilde dropped to one knee and proposed to Constance Lloyd. It was in the same room in which her own parents had become engaged.

At 2.30 pm on 29 May 1889, in St James's Church, Sussex Gardens in Paddington, London, Mr Oscar Fingal O'Flahertie Wills Wilde married Miss Constance Mary Lloyd. Due to illness, Constance's grandfather was unable to attend the wedding so it was up to her uncle to do the honours of giving her away. Their witnesses were Lady Wilde and Oscar's older brother, Willie. It was, by the standards of the day, a small affair and not the 'celebrity' event expected of the dandified Mr Oscar Wilde.

Oscar and Constance choose Paris, the city of Enlightenment, culture and art for their honeymoon. While they enjoyed the romantic city of lights, theirs was not to be a passionate escape for two, as the couple had a full social calendar, attending exhibitions featuring Oscar's friend Whistler, and even seeing the darling of the Victorian stage, Sarah Bernhardt in the opera of *Macbeth*.

Prior to their marriage, with a little financial assistance from Constance's grandfather, John Horatio Lloyd, the couple had managed to secured the lease on their home at 16 Tite Street, Chelsea. The lease was for six years and the couple wanted to make the house their own with renovations. Just seven weeks after Oscar and Constance were married, her grandfather died, leaving Constance the considerable sum of £11,500, making her financially independent.

The work on 16 Tite Street would become expensive and drawn out due to issues with their first builder and delays and added expenditure from the second. As the work went on Oscar left the project in Constance's capable hands as he went to earn an income giving more lectures and talks around the UK and Ireland.

Once she was united to Oscar by marriage, Constance suddenly found herself thrust into the limelight as one of the most talked about 'celebrities' of the day. As a couple they attended opening nights of plays and art exhibitions. But as well as the fun and gaiety that came with being well known, the pair also threw their influence and names behind causes that they were passionate about, including Women's rights and the Women's Dress Reform Movement. Constance for her part would become a minor celebrity in her own right as she became known for her less than conventional dress sense, she abandoned the traditional ridged and structural corsetry of the day.

Despite living busy social lives, both as a couple and separately while Oscar was lecturing, it was not long until Constance fell pregnant with the couple's first child. On 5 June 1885, Constance gave birth to their eldest son, Cyril, at their Tite Street home. It was a typical birth of the time, Constance was aided with the use of forceps while under the influence of chloroform. Both Constance and Oscar doted on the new member of their little family and within nine months of his birth Constance was pregnant again with her second child. It was during her second pregnancy that Oscar stopped feeling sexually attracted to his once slender wife. On 3 November 1886, Constance was delivered of a second son, Vyvyan, and the Wilde family was complete.

It was arguably during this period that Oscar was at the beginning of his most creative and productive work as a journalist. He was also writing short stories and plays. Family life had started to bore him, while his creativity blossomed. His boredom also opened him out to new people and new experiences.

During 1886, 17-year-old Robert Ross would lodge temporarily with Constance and Oscar while his mother went to Europe. Both Constance and Oscar adored the young Ross, however it is thought that during this time, it was Ross that encouraged, seduced and introduced Wilde to the delights and pleasures of homosexual love. Despite his young age, it was Ross who was the teacher, willing to share his experience with the older Wilde.

According to the author of Constance's biography, Franny Moyle, it was around this time that Constance's insecurities about her relationship with Oscar started to show. These were particularly heightened after the birth of Vyvyan in late 1886. However, according to Moyles, Constance did not realise that Oscar's sexual tastes had shifted to men.

It is fair to say that the couple's relationship changed during this time, as they learnt to live with changes within their family dynamic. Despite the change in Oscar's feelings, they remained committed to each other, their love seemed to have shifted from that of passionate lovers to friends; to the outside world, they were still a happy, functioning family unit. This would be reflected in their relationship right up to the time of Constance's death in 1898. The pair remained married; although separated after Oscar's conviction and prison sentence, they never actually divorced.

Wilde managed to keep his affairs discreet and to uphold his family-man image and life; he was, in all senses, having his cake and eating it. This would change when he met one man who would be at the centre of his downfall and consequently affect the lives of both Oscar and Constance. In 1891, Oscar spent most of the first two thirds of the year working on the play that would become known as *Lady Windermere's Fan*. However, he was not so busy during that summer that he did not socialise, and it was at one such social occasion that Oscar was introduced to a student by the name of Lord Alfred Douglas – better known as 'Bosie'.

Having finished writing *Lady Windermere's Fan*, in the autumn of that year, Oscar and his doctors were claiming that he was suffering from bad nerves and exhaustion. His doctor suggested a six-week rest and recuperation. Oscar being Oscar decided that Paris would be the best place for him to recuperate. He would stay in the city of lights until late December 1891 – twelve weeks, rather than the six weeks recommended. While in Paris he managed to write *Salomé*. But in early 1892, when the play was being rehearsed, it was stopped by the Lord Chamberlain's office for being too controversial, it was too sexually explicit for a biblical story and considered blasphemous.

Oscar was by now frustrated both with his work due to the difficulties with *Salomé* as well as the tedium of domestic life. These feelings of frustration meant that he claimed he needed to take another break away from Constance and his family to help with managing his stress. This time he went to the German spa town of Bad Homburg. By some serendipitous turn of events, the student he had met the previous summer, Bosie, also happened to be in that particular German spa town at the same time. The pair became inseparable both in Germany and when they returned to the UK. Details of the friendship between Wilde and Bosie is examined in detail in the following chapter, "A New Awakening".

Oscar would only become a more diligent father and husband at the end of 1893 into early 1894 when Bosie was away from the UK. Bosie telegrammed Constance requesting that she encourage Oscar to visit him as he was now in Paris. We will never know why Constance obliged Bosie and encouraged her husband to visit him, but she did. In February 1894, Oscar joined Bosie in Paris. This reconciliation of the two lovers would start a string of events that would bring about legal actions that would have dire consequences for the whole Wilde family, including Constance.

Constance and Oscar made a pretence of being a happy couple during 1894, but Oscar was away from his family and wife more often than not until Christmas 1894, which would be the last that the Wilde family spent together. Over that festive period of 1894, Oscar was home with his family and Constance was reminded of the man she had married. Ironically, it was during this time that the playwright completed his play *An Ideal Husband*.

Bosie's father, John Sholto Douglas, the Marquess of Queensberry, was like many typical Victorian aristocrats – a misogynist product of the age, and he had very strong feelings regarding effeminacy in men. By today's standards he was a bigot. These feelings of distaste and discrimination would have become heightened when his son Bosie became friendly with Oscar Wilde, the biggest and most notorious dandy of the period, so the marquess started a harassing campaign against Wilde. Relations between Bosie and his father had always been problematic and complicated, but had become much worse by this time in 1894. Bosie loathed his father and, knowing how his father felt, it is highly probable that he used Oscar to further enrage his father. We will never know this for certain, but Bosie was certainly selfish and self-centred enough not to care about the consequences of his actions, in the personal pursuit of harming his father. Constance and the children certainly would never crossed his mind.

Oscar did not take stock of the situation and do the sensible thing; either be far more discreet with Bosie, or part ways with his problematic lover. He was taking a big risk with regard to his career, his reputation, and most crucial of all – his relationship with Constance and his sons. He also hadn't realised that he was gambling with his liberty.

The marquess could not let his son's relationship with Wilde pass without comment, and Oscar finally had to respond to Queensberry's provocation in February 1895. The events leading up to his decision to take the marquess to court are covered in detail later, but the tipping point came when Queensberry decided to prove a point at Oscar's club. He left a calling card for him with the words: 'For Oscar Wilde, posing somdomite [*sic*]'. While doing so, he ensured the staff saw what he had written and asked that it be given to him the next time he visited.

When Wilde received the calling card and its crude message, he consulted his lawyer, Mr Humphreys. Oscar's complaint resulted in a warrant for Queensberry's arrest on 2 March 1895. The arrest of a well known aristocrat quickly made the press and public interest was sparked. Especially as the offended parties were Oscar Wilde and the defendant's own son, Bosie.

Unsurprisingly, Constance's health took a turn for the worse during this time, no doubt exacerbated by the stress of the impending libel trial. Oscar, encouraged by Bosie, decided to celebrate what they thought would be the end of Queensberry by taking a trip to Monte Carlo for a week, leaving Constance and the boys to deal with the savage press attention alone.

The biggest act of support that Constance showed Oscar was on 1 April 1895, when she accompanied him to a performance of *The Importance of Being Earnest*. She walked through the press and fans at the front of the theatre arm-in-arm with Oscar in a brave act of defiance.

The trial of Queensberry started on 3 April 1895 at the Old Bailey. Unfortunately for Oscar, Queensberry's legal team had been very efficient. The evidence presented by Queensberry's lawyers was beyond damning. The bulk of the evidence had been found by a private investigator, who had tracked down a number of rent boys that Wilde and Bosie had frequented. Fuller details of the trials appear in later chapters of the book. After three days of hearing sordid evidence, Wilde decided to withdraw the charges against Queensberry. For all intents and purposes, he was publicly admitting that the damning evidence was true.

In an act of cowardice, Oscar left Robbie Ross, his first male lover and subsequently his most loyal friend, to tell Constance what had happened at the Old Bailey. Constance had thankfully been absent from the court hearing due to being bedbound through sickness. She, like Oscar, must have realised that he was now in danger of being prosecuted for gross indecency, and this would affect not just his ability to work, but her reputation and the lives of their two young sons.

This crisis was made even worse by the new financial burden caused by the failed court case. Wilde was left to pay the court charges, which came to the princely sum of £700. The family were already in a tight financial situation despite the fact that Wilde had two successful plays running in the theatre at this time.

Then, at 6.30 pm on 6 April 1895, Oscar was arrested on multiple charges of gross indecency. The failed libel case had provided the Crown with enough extremely damning evidence to bring criminal charges against Oscar. This must have been embarrassing and humiliating for Constance, both privately and socially. This public humiliation was made worse by the content of both the domestic and European press over the coming weeks. This must have been unbearable for poor Constance. As the scandal around Oscar deepened, many former allies of both Constance and Oscar distanced themselves from their association with the Wildes; just at the point when Constance needed good friends. Thankfully, for the most part, the general public, the press and most of her friends and family saw Constance and the boys as the victims of this sensational scandal. Constance even received numerous letters of support, including from passing acquaintances and total strangers.

After Oscar was arrested and held on remand, Constance's first priority was her sons. She had taken both boys out of school when the libel case had started and she had sent Cyril to her family in Ireland. She had decided to kept her youngest and more delicate son Vyvyan with her in London. Constance decided that the best course of action for her and the boys was to separate from Oscar. As if things were not bad enough, Constance now found herself harassed by Oscar's many creditors, all demanding money for his debts. On 24 April 1895, the content of the Wilde's family home on Tite Street, was auctioned off cheaply to help cover Oscar's growing debts. It was not just Oscar's possessions that were sold off; private letters Constance had received from Oscar, the valuable first additions of his books, and even the children's toys, were all sold to appease his creditors.

Two days later, on 26 April 1895, Oscar's trial started. Cyril returned from his family visit in Ireland in early May and through the generosity of friends and family, Constance was able to hire a governess and send the boys to Europe, away from the scandal of their father's trial and vicious press coverage. They would settle in the Swiss Alps with the governess as Constance started sorting out her own future and affairs in London. One of the things to sort out was a legal separation from Oscar; however, upon seeking legal advice, she was told that the best course of action for both her and the boys' future was to file for divorce instead. Constance was less comfortable with this course of action. She clearly still cared about her estranged husband despite the way he had behaved and the scandal he had brought upon them as a family. By 25 May 1895 Oscar had been found guilty by the jury of his trial for committing acts of gross indecency.

Oscar was allowed to write one letter a month and have one visitor a month in the early days of his sentence at HMP Wandsworth. He used that first letter to write to Constance asking her to forgive him and reconsider divorcing him. It is worth noting the divorce never happened, even if it would have been better financially for her boys' future. She did not, however, keep Wilde's surname, choosing to take an old family name, Holland, for the rest of her life and her boys' lives. Constance and the boys enjoyed the rest of the summer of 1895, in Switzerland. The Hollands were joined by Otho and his family.

At the end of that summer, the boys were sent to their Uncle Otho in Switzerland so that Constance could return to England to visit Oscar in gaol. Much campaigning and letter writing had taken place to enable her to make this visit. On 21 September, Constance entered Wandsworth Prison to visit the man she had married. Whatever her expectations, she had clearly not imagined the reality of a prison visit. She was unable to actually see Oscar, and there was absolutely no question of the two touching. The visit left her less hopeful and despairing for her husband's welfare.

After her brief journey back to London, Constance rejoined her brother and the boys in Switzerland. Her next task was to start to bring some normality back to the boys' lives. This meant they needed to restart their abandoned education. Initially, they were home tutored by their Uncle Otho, and this continued until early 1896. Constance and the boys then left her brother's family and relocated to the north of Italy, primarily for the slightly better climate for her poor health. In this new home, based in north Italy near Genoa, Constance found an expat community which included some of the Pre-Raphaelites, including Oscar's friend, John Ruskin. Ruskin had befriended Constance after her marriage to Wilde. Unfortunately, Constance's health issues would come to dominate this last part of her short life.

Constance had had delicate health as a child, but her serious health problems began around 1889. By February 1893, she and her doctors were describing her health deterioration and unexplained pain, 'neuralgia', in what is left of her surviving correspondence with her friends and family. Her health had been relatively stable until early 1895 when she started having additional mobility issues, brought about by a fall down the stairs at Tite Street. These problems were ongoing when Wilde was arrested.

If Constance had chosen Italy for its Mediterranean sunshine to help ease her poor health, this did not go to plan; the warmer climate did not alleviate the pain and discomfort from her physical illnesses. By the end of that very stressful year of 1895, as she was starting her new life away from scandal, she described her condition as 'lame', because she was struggling with her mobility again. In December of that year, she underwent surgery in Genoa, the nature of which is not clear from the evidence in her correspondence. Initially after the surgery during early 1896, it seems as if the treatment she had received had helped, but this improvement did not last long. By April of 1896, she was once again describing her physical mobility as lame.

Constance was determined to find a doctor that could help her. Between April and October 1896 she sought advice from a specialist in Germany. The paper trail has not left the German doctor's name in letters unfortunately, but we do know that this doctor recommended treatments such as spa baths and electrotherapeutic cures popular and en vogue during this late Victorian age.

During early 1896, Constance was well enough to travel from Italy back to England in order to visit Oscar in Reading gaol, to where he had been transferred in November 1895, in order to break the news of his mother's death to him in person. Willie, his older brother had no stomach to do this sad duty, he claimed Oscar would not wish to see him, though this was probably just an excuse as he did not wish to set foot inside of a prison. Instead, he had contacted his estranged sister-in-law, who was in ill health and living in Europe to do this.

By the end of 1896, Constance had developed a tremor in her right arm. This tremor was so prominent that she was forced to give up hand-writing her letters and took to using a typewriter instead. It was also around this time that she started to suffer from acute headaches and unexplained exhaustion. The mental stress of this situation she was already in must have been great, but to be suffering from these debilitating physical symptoms, that no doctor seemed to know the cause of or how to treat, was yet another burden she had to cope with all alone. It was her love for Cyril and Vyvyan that drove her to keep looking for a cure.

As Constance neared the end of her life, the right-hand side of her face suffered facial paralysis. Given all her symptoms over the latter half of her life, *The Lancet* medical journal concluded that the former she may have suffered from Multiple Sclerosis. This modern postmortem diagnosis certainly explains Constance's pain and exhaustion, and why she had some short periods of relief when her symptoms were less severe. The facial paralysis may have been the result of a mild stroke. Realistically, we can never know the exact cause of her illness.

In the final months of her life Constance was afflicted with further discomfort and pain with genitourinary disease which covers issues affecting kidneys, bladder and genitals. Constance underwent treatment consisting of antiseptic pessaries. Given that forceps were used to assist the birth of her children, this may have caused damage which contributed or possibly caused some of these issues. When the pessaries failed to treat her new symptoms, she was persuaded to undertake surgery. Given her poor health generally and the time period, this was always going to be a risky course of action to take. The risk was such that both her

London and German doctors tried to dissuade her from undertaking the procedure – advice she chose to ignore. Given all these risks, Constance had the operation on 2 April 1898 and came through it alive. The doctors decided not to perform a full hysterectomy and instead performed a myomectomy that removed only her uterine fibroids instead.

For the first few days after her surgery, Constance recuperated well. This would change on the fourth day when she started to vomit, which in turn caused serious dehydration. Given her already poor health, she grew weaker and weaker until she became unconscious, and then died on 7 April 1898. According to *The Lancet*, it is believe she died of severe paralytic ileus, a condition that occurs within the intestines, when the muscles become paralysed, preventing the passage of food. The causes of paralytic ileus, can be caused by many different reasons but in Constance's case, the most likely cause was due to the surgery.

No matter how you look at it, this was a tragic end for a woman who had endured much in life, both privately and publicly. She was only 40 years old when she died leaving her two young sons without a mother. Constance never did get her sought after fresh start and new beginning when she relocated from London. Although she and Oscar separated, they didn't divorce and remained on mostly civil terms; an achievement not all of us could manage in her situation and under the scrutiny of the public eye.

A NEW AWAKENING

'Selfishness is not living as one wishes to live,
it is asking others to live as one wishes to live.'

Oscar Wilde

The true understanding of another person's emotional feelings and sexuality is something only they can truly understand and experience during their lifetime. We are fortunate to live during times where conversations about sexuality and identity can be had freely and openly, and there is generally greater empathy in Western society. Wilde was not so lucky, just as many around the world today are equally discriminated against, for the simple reason of loving someone of the same gender. Any examination to seek the *real* Oscar Wilde, needs to explore this aspect of the man as well as the important men whom he loved.

Although he was a Victorian, Oscar Wilde was by no means ignorant of 'the love that shall not speak its name'. First, Wilde and his brother attended a boys' boarding school, the Portora Royal School in Enniskillen, County Fermanagh. Wilde described this aspect of his schooldays with his friend and biographer, Frank Harris in chapter 18 of *Oscar Wilde, His life and Confessions*:

> Of course I was sensual and curious as boys are; and I had the usual boy imaginings; but I did not indulge in them excessively. At Portora … nearly everyone went in for athletics – running and jumping and so forth; no one appeared to care for sex. We were healthy young barbarians.

Although he may not have indulged in mutual schoolboy sexual exploration, it was at school that Oscar received a Classical education and learnt about all aspects of the Classical world and language, particularly looking at ancient Greek culture. In his final year at Portora he won a scholarship on the back of his excellent knowledge of Classics. Through these studies and his vast extra reading on the subject Wilde would have learnt about the Greek tradition of pederasty – a word used in derogatory terms today. This was the Greek tradition of an older male mentoring a younger male in exchange for sexual favours. In Ancient Greece this was not seen as wrong or as abuse, but as a coming of age, a rite of passage that benefited both parties. It is not therefore unreasonable to assume that later in life, Oscar saw himself as an older mentor to some of his younger male lovers – particularly in relation to Robert Ross – There is more about 'Robbie' Ross later in the chapter.

His study of Greek language, culture and history continued into his university education first at Trinity College Dublin, and then at Oxford University at Magdalen Collage. Again, there is no evidence of homosexual or even heterosexual relationships while Oscar was at university. He had, at this time started to develop his aesthetic persona and in doing so may have alluded to an eccentric, flamboyant even effeminate side of his personality, displayed through his style of dress and the decor of his rooms at the college. At this time all universities were only open for male students and he did develop several strong male friendships with the Harding brothers James and Reginald, and David Hunter-Blair. Although their friendships were close, there is no hint that they were anything other than platonic in nature.

During his university years outside of term time Wilde had romantic interests in several young women, one being Florence Balcombe who was the daughter of an Army Lieutenant-Colonel. Wilde described Florence to Harding as 'The most perfectly beautiful face I ever saw and not a sixpence of money.' Florence Balcombe would eventually marry fellow Irish writer and acquaintance Bram Stoker. Wilde and his 'Florrie' had not been romantically associated for some time but it is said that upon hearing of the couple's engagement, he wallowed in heartache for a few days. In a letter dated 30 September 1878 to Florence, Wilde requests that she return a small gold cross he had given her:

> I need hardly say that I would not ask it from you if it was anything you valued, but worthless though the trinket be, to me it serves as a memory of two sweet years – the sweetest of all the years of my youth – and I should like to have it always with me .... Though you have not thought it worth while to let me know of your marriage, I still cannot leave Ireland without sending you my wishes that you may be happy.

Another possible, if slightly cliched, indication of Oscar's true self may be the fact that he was naturally drawn towards artistic, creative and literary people. This, of course, started as a boy, when he and Willie mingled at the salons held by their mother in their Merrion Square home in Dublin. He could have become a writer of any genre, but Wilde's greatest works are written for the stage – another safer environment for the Victorian queer community.

One of the first reasons Wilde was considered effeminate was due to his long hair and aesthetic and unique dress sense. He broke rigid social Victorian codes of dress, wearing his hair longer at a time the fashion for men was short hair, was clean shaven when men favoured whiskers, moustaches and beards. He chose luxurious fabrics such as fur and velvet, in non-traditional colours such as purple. As a student in Oxford he stood out from his peers by wearing knee breeches from his Masonry regalia as daily wear. This was a trend he continued to wear into the first half of his American lecture tour in 1882. This sense of unique style and going against tradition and social norms drew attention to him, and then caused less open or friendly minds to cast aspersions upon his possible sexual inclinations.

But it was not until 1886, when Oscar met a 17-year-old youth who would change his life and be his most loyal friend and confidant; the youth was Robert ('Robbie') Ross. Exactly how Oscar and Robbie first met has never been clarified by either Ross or Wilde, but like Wilde, Ross loved literature and art, moved in well-connected circles and was based in London in 1886. Ross had moved from Canada with his mother and elder sisters at the age of 2 after the death of his father. In 1886, Ross was preparing for the entry examinations for Cambridge. By the age of 17, Ross had not only accepted his sexuality but was also sexually experienced. It may have been their love of literature and art that brought them together, but it was Ross, not Wilde, that did the seducing. It is unlikely that Wilde needed much encouragement. As mentioned before, given Wilde's love of Greek history and his tastes in literature, that he may have been curious about homosexuality and its physical side. Wilde, with his overly romanticising nature and imagination, would have likely felt that the new delightful pleasure he had discovered brought him closer to understanding the homosexual artistic elites such as Michaelangelo and Da Vinci.

The sexual element of Oscar and Robbie's relationship did not last long, but their friendship would be life long, loyal and affectionate; Wilde was lucky to have had Ross as his friend when many others distanced themselves from him.

A letter from Oscar to Ross dated 13 October 1888 is telling of his affection for his new acquaintance: 'My Dear Bobbie, I congratulate you. University life will suit you admirably though I shall miss you in town.' He ends the letter 'Ever Yours Oscar Wilde' (*The Complete Letters of Oscar Wilde*, Holland and Hart p.360). Indeed, the pair were on Christmas gift-giving terms and it seems that Ross gave the Wilde family a kitten for Christmas of 1888. In a letter to Ross from late December 1888 Wilde writes:

December 1888,   16 Tite Street

My Dear Bobbie, the kitten is quite lovely. It does not look white, indeed it looks a sort of tortoise-shell colour or grey barred with velvety dark brown, but as you said it was white I have given orders that it is always to be spoken of as the 'white kitten'. The children are enchanted with it.

Oscar had intimate relationships with many men, as the transcriptions from his trials reveal. Several of those young men were rent boys and found on nights out with Bosie. Prior to meeting Bosie it is known that Wilde was linked with Marc-André Raffalovich, a 22-year-old Russian Banker; John Ehret Dickenson, a wealthy son of a paper manufacturer; the artist W Graham Robertson; Arthur Clifton, a solicitor and eager supporter of Liberal politics, to name but a few. But the young man who would be his ultimate downfall was yet to be met.

Oscar was introduced to Lord Alfred Douglas, who was better known by his family monicker of Bosie, at the end of June 1891. The introduction was made by Lionel Johnson, who brought Douglas to the Wilde family home upon Bosie's insistence. To say that the then 20-year-old Bosie was a fan of Wilde's work was an understatement. He boasted to anyone who would listen that he had read *The Picture of Dorian Gray* through several times. Both Johnson and Douglas were under graduates at Oxford and had gone to the Winchester public school together. Their relationship was a sexual one and had been since their schooldays.

From that first meeting, Wilde found the young Lord Douglas to have been very aesthetically pleasing, with his youthful looks, golden blonde hair and slender figure. Douglas was also very charming and engaging in conversation. Like Wilde he was an Oxford man and he aspired to be a great poet. He was also knowledgeable and highly flattering about Wilde's works. When Wilde introduced Bosie to Constance, he was polite and charmed her, leaving a positive first impression on both of the Wildes.

Wilde and Bosie lunched together several days after that first meeting at the Lyric club. He also presented Douglas with an inscribed copy of *The Picture of Dorian Gray*. The inscription said: 'Alfred Douglas, from his friend who wrote this book, Oscar 91 July.' At this point Wilde hinted that he would have liked to have taken Douglas as his lover, however Wilde was too old for Douglas's tastes and their friendship developed slowly and platonically over the summer of 1891, and then Bosie returned to Oxford and his studies. It was not until the spring of 1892, that the dynamics of the relationship would change and show Oscar the true behaviour and nature of Bosie.

In spring 1892, Wilde received a letter from Bosie appealing to Oscar for help, as he was being blackmailed. The exact details of what he was being blackmailed over has never been clarified, but given that he went to Wilde for help, rather than his family, implies that he was being blackmailed over some sort of sexual indiscretion with a male.

Given that Wilde and Douglas had only met a few times over the previous summer and were not great friends at this point – it was quite presumptuous that he decided to write to Oscar in order to enlist his help in this mess. Oscar being Oscar, he felt sorry for the youth and set about helping him. The first thing he did was put Bosie in touch with George Lewis, who specialised in dodging scandal. They then brought in the professional services of one Edwin Levy, a private detective, who helped Wilde pay off the blackmailers, £100. Levy could see exactly the type of man Douglas was and he tried to warn the infatuated Wilde that Bosie was trouble. Wilde was not to be persuaded.

After Wilde had saved him, Douglas become far more open to Wilde's overtures to making their relationship sexual. This longed-for conquest happened in the spring/summer of 1892, one night when Constance and the boys were away. Wilde brought Bosie back to the family home on Tite Street. It had certainly happened by late May or early June 1892, as Wilde writes to Robbie Ross: 'Bosie is so tired: he lies like a hyacinth on the sofa and I worship him.'

The Wilde family summer holiday that year was taken in Cromer in the county of Norfolk. During this holiday Wilde worked on *A Woman of No Importance*, as well as taking up golf. The two boys, Cyril and Vyvyan, were located in Cambridgeshire convalescing from a bout of whooping cough. Constance stayed with Oscar for a month before she returned to London. Oscar was then accompanied by Bosie, who had invited himself to stay for a night and then just didn't leave. During this time Oscar learnt about Bosie's promiscuity and his frequent use of rent boys and male prostitutes in London.

This new exciting prospect of meeting beautiful young men had piqued Wilde's interest, and by October 1892 Bosie had help initiate Wilde to this underground gay subculture in Victorian London. The pimp Wilde was introduced to was named Alfred Taylor. On this first invitation Taylor had found a young man who worked as a clerk by day and rent boy by night; his name was Sidney Mavour.

The encounter had such an impact on Wilde, that he sent Mr Mavour a generous gift of silver cigarette case engraved with the following: 'Sidney from OW October 1892'. This was a typical over-generous gesture on Oscar's part, and it would ultimately become a habit for him to gift silver cigarette cases to the men he slept with; unfortunately these kinds of gifts, engraved with his initials or name, would be used as evidence in court in 1895.

After introducing Wilde to Taylor, the relationship between Bosie and Oscar altered, certainly on Bosie's part. They remained great friends and even occasionally slept together, but now they had the new, thrilling pastime of picking up rent boys. It was this new pastime, that meant the two friends were often seen together in and around London, dining and drinking, and so their friendship was brought to the attention of Bosie's father, the Marquess of Queensberry.

Oscar, it seems, was still bewitched by his 'honey haired boy', evident in a letter to Bosie of January 1893: 'My Own Boy, Your sonnet is quite lovely, and it is a marvel that those red rose leaf lips of yours should have been made no less for music of song than for madness of kisses.'

Initially, the marquess decided to air his concerns about with Wilde to his estranged son in a letter, asking him to end his friendship with the poet. Bosie ignored his father's request. A few days after this letter was sent, Wilde and Bosie were having lunch at Cafe Royal, when the marquess entered the restaurant. Upon seeing his father, Bosie actually invited him to join them for lunch. Wilde's wit and charm momentarily won the marquess over. It is therefore hard to believe that within eighteen months of this lunch, the marquess had started a terrible public campaign of hate directed at Wilde that would end up bringing both sides to court, and eventually end in Wilde's conviction and imprisonment for gross indecency. Evidence of the Marquess of Queensberry's persecution of Wilde can be found in a letter from Oscar to Bosie in the late summer of 1894:

> Your father is on the rampage again – been to Cafe Royal to enquire for us, with threats etc. I think now it would have been better for me to have had him bound over to keep the peace, but what a scandal! Still it is intolerable to be dogged by a maniac.

Given Oscar's knowledge and love for ancient Greece and its history, it is reasonable to presume that if Robbie Ross had not seduced him then another male would have at some point. This new sexual liberation, came at a time when his career was starting to succeed – he was having his cake and eating it. It is just a shame that fate would not allow this new happiness personally and professionally to last.

OSCAR WILDE'S POLITICS

'I adore political parties. They are the only places left to us
where people don't talk politics.'
An Ideal Husband, Oscar Wilde

Like many of Oscar Wilde's core beliefs, his politics were being shaped at an early age by his mother, Lady Jane Wilde, through her literary salons as well as her writings and poetry. Living in nineteenth-century Dublin, the Wildes were part of the British Empire, Victoria was their Queen, and yet Lady Wilde – like many fellow Irish men and women – felt that they were Irish and should have an independent country away from the British Empire. Ireland had an independent history, language, faith and culture that flourished before becoming part of the British Empire.

This Irish nationalism became known as the Irish Question and was truthfully defined by the future British Prime Minister, Benjamin Disraeli in 1844:

> That dense population in extreme distress inhabited an island where there was an established church; and a territorial aristocracy, the richest of whom lived in distinct capitals. Thus they had a starving population, an absentee aristocracy, and an alien church and in addition the weakest executive in the world, that was the Irish Question.
>
> Benjamin Disraeli,
> 16 February 1844,
> State of Ireland Parliamentary debate

The Irish Question had a long and bloody history with consequences that affected the people of Ireland well into the late twentieth century. It was a problem that had started in the sixteenth century and had caused hardship and resentment from the native Irish living under British rule.

Wilde was unusual in that although born in Dublin and an Irishman, his family belonged to the protestant minority, his father was knighted and held an honorary position in Queen Victoria's court as her appointed Oculist-in-ordinary, and yet both Sir William and Lady Jane Wilde wrote passionately about Ireland – Lady Wilde in more political terms than her husband.

Oscar Wilde's views on the Irish Question are apparent in a couple of talks he gave in 1882 during his tour of America; 17 March, at Saint Paul, Minnesota:

> The generous response you have given to the mention of my mother in Ireland's cause, has filled me with a pleasure and pride that I cannot properly acknowledge. It is also a pleasure to me that I am afforded this opportunity during my visit to America to speak to an audience of my countrymen, a race once the most artistic in Europe.
>
> There was a time before the time of Henry II when Ireland stood at the front of all nations of Europe in the arts, the sciences and general intellectually ... there was a time, too, when Ireland was the university of Europe – when young monks educated in Ireland went forth as educators to all other European countries while .... Students from these same countries flocked to Ireland to study arts etc under the great masters of Ireland .... These proud monuments to the genius and intellectuality of Ireland do not exist today. When the English came they were burned.

A damning view of the British overlords, eloquently expressed. Wilde never lived to see Irish Home Rule become a reality, to see the heroism and passion of those who fought for an independent Ireland in the early part of twentieth century, when the whole world was changing and recovering after the bloody events of the First World War (1914–1918) and the slow decline of the British Empire.

Lady Wilde did not just instil national politics to her sons. She had her own views on women's suffrage, reform and women's rights, which were also highlighted to her boys through the people she invited to her literary salons. One of these courageous women who came to lady Wilde's salon was Millicent Fawcett. Lady Jane was far from conventional; she had married late and was far more outspoken and liberal than many of her peers, even after her marriage.

Wilde was clearly influenced by his mother's teaching when he chose Constance Lloyd for his wife. Constance was intelligent, spirited, and not the usual Victorian woman who lived to marry, have children and serve her husband. After their marriage Constance would become involved not just in her husband's life and causes, but was also involved with her own charities and good causes.

One cause that both Mr and Mrs Wilde were happy to support was the women's dress reform movement through involvement with the Rational Dress Society. For his part Oscar wrote several letters in 1884 to the *Pall Mall Gazette* about how women should dress. He believed women should be comfortable and even suggested divided skirts, like wide legged culottes that looked like a skirt, but were in fact trousers. This would free women from petticoats. Women's dress reform would become one of Constance's good causes which she used her new celebrity status to promote. One way she was able to do this was to lead by example and wear less restrictive clothing.

Oscar would tackle such issues when he took over the editorship of *The Woman's World*, and one of the people he asked to contribute was Millicent Fawcett:

> Let no man or woman be mistaken as to what this movement
> for women's suffrage really means. We none of us want
> to turn the world up-side down or to convert women into

men. We want women, on the contrary, above all things to continue womanly … and bring their true woman's influence on behalf of whatever things are true, honest, just, pure, lovely and of good report, to bear upon the conduct of public affairs.

The Woman's World, Volume II, pp.9–12

To publish such an article in a magazine aimed at women was a bold move. Wilde was strong enough in his political convictions to do this, and to ensure that women knew they were important to the political landscape and should fight for equal rights.

In 1891, Oscar wrote a political essay called 'Soul of Man Under Socialism'. The piece is anti-capitalist and a rejection of privately owned property. He points out that although well meaning, charity is not a solution to poverty but rather an enabler; what is needed is political and social reform. He argues that these changes would produce more individualism and create an equal society, which in turn would create greater freedom of thought and more widespread art and critical thinking.

Wilde was expressing fairly radical views in this essay, the Victorian age was capitalist, it was authoritarian, it had well defined social classes and what it perceived as order. Wilde's views may not have been as fiery as Karl Marx's socialism, but it these views were idealistic libertarian, examining not just politics and society, but each individual's soul. Wilde felt that capitalism did not permit the poorest people in society to help themselves out of poverty or to improve themselves.

Although Wilde clearly put thought into these ideas and theories he was not exactly living a socialist lifestyle. Born into a wealthy family that paid for him to be educated, he was able to attend two universities; he travelled as a child, as a student and as an adult and he married into wealth – had he not been so extravagant and over-generous, the Wildes could have lived well within their means.

At the end of his life, it is fair to say that Wilde relied very heavily upon the generosity and charity given to him by friends, as he struggled to settle into life in exile following his release from prison. Frank Harris and Robbie Ross frequently received letters begging for money. If we were to apply Wilde's own message from his essay of 1891, his friends were not helping Wilde, but enabling him to remain poor. This is why political theories are problematic – it is easy to be excited about them when you are not the one struggling to survive.

Although Aestheticism shared some of these social principles, mainly that society focused too much on making money to survive than allowing the mind meet its artistic and intellectual needs. The only people who could fully meet the needs of their minds were those who had independent means to enable them to write or create art. Again, Wilde fell into that category of being comfortable enough to be able to focus more on his art than making money.

Towards the end of his life, and having been through the hard realities of the Victorian prison system, Wilde used his name, notoriety and experiences to make public the need for reform.

The day before he was released from prison, three small children were brought into Reading Gaol, the youngest was very small. Wilde was so moved by these children that he set about securing their release. He found out a few weeks later, while he was in exile, that one of the wardens had been sacked for giving the smallest child a biscuit. The letter he wrote to the editor of the *Daily Chronicle* on 27 May 1897 shows not just his empathy, but a modern understanding of prison, of children in prison, and the need for reform:

> to shut up a child in a dimly lit cell, for twenty-three hours out of the twenty-our, is an example of the cruelty of stupidity. If an individual, parent or guardian, did this to a child, he would be severely punished. The Society for the Prevention of Cruelty to Children would take the matter up at once. ... but our own actual society does worse itself, and to the child to be treated by a strange abstract force, of whose claims it has no cognisance, is much worse than it would be to receive the same treatment from its father or mother ... the inhuman treatment of a child is always inhuman.

Wilde wrote to the editor of the *Daily Chronicle* again ten months later on 23 March 1898, ahead of the Prison Reform Bill being read to parliament. Once again he uses his name and first-hand experience in his passionate letter to the editor:

> The necessary reforms are very simple. They concern the needs of the body and the needs of the minds of each unfortunate prisoner. With regards to the first, there are three permanent punishments authorised by law in English prisons:
>
> 1. Hunger
> 2. Insomnia
> 3. Disease
>
> The food supplied to prisoners is entirely inadequate. ... the result of the food – which in most cases consists of weak gruel, badly baked bread suet, and water – is disease in the form of incessant diarrhoea. ... Nothing can be worse than the sanitary arrangements of English prisons ... a small tin vessel is supplied to each prisoner ... A man suffering from diarrhoea is consequently placed in a position so loathsome that it is unnecessary to dwell on it.

These eloquent letters show us that the real Oscar Wilde was politically savvy and a highly empathetic man. He was ahead of his time in many of the political and social theories and causes he supported and championed. Many of these issues are still relevant today, from women's rights, to understanding the best way to deal with children and adults who have broken the law. The fact that he was willing to use his own experiences to help bring about change and reform says a lot about his character.

THE SCARLET MARQUESS'S PURSUIT 1894-5

'Every single human being should
be the fulfilment of a prophecy.'
De Profundis, Oscar Wilde

The next part of Wilde's life would be dominated by non-stop harassment from Bosie's father, that would eventually end up in court for both parties.

John Sholto Douglas, 9th Marquess of Queensberry was born on 20 July 1844. Due to his inherited title, he was a peer of Scotland and was nominated by his fellow peers to go down to London to sit in the House of Lords as a Scottish representative peer, which he did until 1880, when he refused to take a religious oath of allegiance as he was an agnostic.

Queensberry was brutish, homophobic, an absent father (according to Bosie), misogynistic, ill-tempered and stubborn. He divorced Bosie's mother – Sibyl Montgomery – in 1887 and later married Ethel Weeden in 1893. This marriage ended in annulment the following year.

One the marquess's biggest passions was sport, in particular boxing. He left his mark upon the sport by having the rules named after him, they would become known as 'The Marquess of Queensberry Rules'.

The marquess's harassment of his Bosie and Wilde really took hold in 1894. In spring of that year, the marquess had written to his estranged son demanding that he cut ties with Wilde as had become aware of their close friendship and rumours of Wilde's sexuality. Within this letter his father threaten to cut off Bosie's allowance. Of course, Bosie fired an angry letter back saying that he was of age and could do as he pleased as well as befriend whomever he pleased.

A couple of weeks later, Queensberry spotted his son and Wilde lunching at Cafe Royal. Bosie invited his father over to join them and by all accounts it was a pleasant lunch, with good conversation had by all. Bosie even left his father and Wilde to talk when the conversation turned to religion. But despite the pleasant lunch the marquess once again wrote to his son: 'With my own eyes I saw you both in the most loathsome and disgusting relationship as expressed by your manner and expression … Also I now hear on good authority, but this may [be] false, that his wife is petitioning to divorce him for sodomy and other crimes.' (Sturgis, *Oscar, a life* p.501)

By the beginning of May, the pair had planned a trip to Tuscany via Paris, where the pair socialised and enjoyed the city of Renaissance art, Florence. Wilde returned to London on 1 June where he could often be found in Cafe Royal surrounded by young artistic groupies. While Wilde was living his best life, the marquess was plotting to break up his son's friendship with Wilde. He started this by employing a private detective by the name of Cook, to follow Wilde.

Up until then, the marquess's threats and unpleasant comments had been directed only at his son, but of course Wilde had been informed of Queensberry's vendetta against him from Bosie. On 30 June 1894, the Marquess of Queensberry, accompanied by a thug, were waiting in Wilde's library at Tite Street. Wilde returned home at 4 pm and was informed he had a visitor. It was by no means a friendly visit. Thinking fast, Wilde started the conversation by provoking the marquess, demanding to know if Queensberry was there to apologise to Wilde for the vicious and vindictive comments in his letters to Bosie and expressing that his wife was divorcing him for sodomy. During the exchange Wilde realised that the marquess had been having him followed, as he seemed to know details of his recent movements around London and who he had been with. Wilde recalls how aggressively irate the marquess became during their exchange. Part of the vicious and angry exchange is quoted in Sturgis's biography: 'If I catch you and my son together in any public restaurant, I will thrash you!' Wilde replied, 'I don't know what the Queensberry rules are, but the Oscar Wilde rule is to shoot at sight.' (Sturgis, *Oscar,* p.508)

With that parting blow from Wilde, he instructed his butler to throw the marquess and his thug out, telling the staff never to let him in to the house again. When Bosie heard of the meeting, he was of course outraged and became even more determined to find a way to hit back at his father. For Wilde, the easiest solution would have been to cool off relations with Bosie, but Oscar was never one for the easiest solution and he was beyond smitten with his 'honey haired boy' and unwilling to break their connection.

Learning of her ex-husband's behaviour, the former Lady Queensberry, advised and cautioned Wilde not to pursue the marquess through legal means – advice that Wilde chose to ignore, and was encouraged by Bosie to do so. As the marquess had invaded his family home, Wilde felt that legal action, even via a solicitor's letter, was the only option open to him to deal with Queensberry. He got in touch with George Lewis, with whom he had used previously, to seek legal advice. Unfortunately, at this time Lewis had Queensberry as a client and informed Wilde that although he could not advise Oscar, he would not act against him either – he would be a neutral party.

Oscar then sought the help from Mr Charles Humphreys of C.O. Humphreys, Son and Kershaw, as recommended by Robbie Ross. Mr Humphreys senior sent the marquess a letter requesting that he retract the allegations made in his letters to Bosie about Wilde and the state of his marriage. Naturally, the marquess refused to do so and his next move was to start going to all of Bosie and Wilde's favourite places, in the hope to catch them and make a public scene. All the while, Bosie continued to provoke his father via letter.

It was due to this disagreement that Bosie took to carrying a loaded gun with him. Unsurprisingly, an accident happened when the firearm was discharged in the Berkley by mistake. No one was hurt but Bosie handed the weapon in to the authorities.

Queensberry's obsession with Oscar and his son intensified. It started to dominate his life. Wilde reported this obsessional behaviour towards him in several letters to Bosie. This also encouraged Oscar's friends to advise him to distance himself from Bosie. Among those advising this course of action was Reggie Turner and Robbie Ross. Wilde stubbornly refused to do so, he did not see why he should do what Queensberry wanted, and he loved Bosie.

For the rest of that summer of 1894, Lady Queensberry – with the help of Bosie's cousin Wilfrid Blunt – kept Bosie out of London and the gaze of his irate and unstable father, and away from Wilde. The cousins headed to Stratford-upon-Avon, among other places.

This time away from Bosie allowed Wilde to work on what would become *The Importance of Being Earnest* and *An Ideal Husband*, the second play's title being somewhat ironic, given Wilde's behaviour. This writing started first at his family home in Tite Street, and then from mid-August onwards, while on the family summer holiday in Worthing, West Sussex. The family were soon joined by Bosie, despite Constance's unhappiness at this situation. Together, Wilde and Bosie went sailing and picked up local teenage boys together. Bosie departed in early September. Wilde was left not long after by Constance and the boys in order to get them ready for the next school year.

Wilde did not manage to get much more writing done before Bosie reappeared. The pair of them took a ferry over to Dieppe for several days. Around this time a book by an anonymous author entitled *The Green Carnation* appeared and seemed to be a satire of Wilde and Bosie's relationship. The book became known to Queensberry and served only to increase his hatred of Wilde even further. Bosie once again departed Worthing, this time only for a week before returning at the very end of September 1894. The pair decided to relocate to the far busier and noisier Sussex town of Brighton. Upon arrival, Bosie fell ill with influenza. Oscar proceeded to nurse his friend which inevitably led to Oscar also succumbing to influenza. Bosie, however, was less understanding and left Wilde to care for himself in Brighton. When he returned, an argument erupted and Bosie flew into rage calling Wilde selfish to expect him to nurse him when he was ill. The argument was restarted the following day. Wilde, who always disliked confrontations, walked away from this angry Bosie and went to sit in the communal area of the hotel. He hoped that this would help to calm Bosie down. Instead the angry Bosie ransacked Wilde's room looking for any money left about, before departing the hotel and leaving without an apology for even a goodbye.

This incident should have been the end of their association, Wilde was greatly disturbed and hurt by Bosie's behaviour in Brighton. Once he had recovered, he made up his mind to ask his solicitor to write to the marquess, confirming that the pair were no longer friends. However this did not happen, and fate had other plans.

Upon returning to London, Wilde discovered that Bosie's older brother, Lord Drumlanrig had died on a shooting trip in Somerset. His death look much like suicide. Wilde immediately telegrammed Bosie to offer his condolences and their friendship was repaired with no mention of Bosie's outburst and bad behaviour.

In December of 1894, *An Ideal Husband* went into rehearsals for an early 1895 opening at the Haymarket Theatre in London. The play opened on 3 January 1895. Wilde had to attend the first night without poor Constance who had been seriously unwell over the festive period. She had fallen down the stairs at Tite Street and walking had become very painful for her. She was instead being cared for by her friend, Lady Mount Temple, at her home in Babbacombe.

Wilde decided not to reside in the family home but instead took up rooms at the Hotel Albemarle. Here he was able to celebrate the success of the first night of *An Ideal Husband*, with his friends. Professionally, everything was going so well. During the early part of the run for *An Ideal Husband*, there had been a new run of Wilde's earlier play, *Lady Windermere's Fan*. Also at this time the St James's Theatre approached him about putting *The Importance of Being Earnest* on as Henry James's play, *Guy Domville* had been a commercial flop and had closed. *The Importance of Being Earnest* went into rehearsals almost straight away, and opened at the St James's Theatre on Valentine's day, 1895.

Wilde found himself in a better place financially and was eager to spend his earnings. Bosie, too, was excited about this new income that he could manipulate and access via Wilde. So when Bosie suggested that they take a winter break to Algeria, it took very little to persuade Wilde it was a good idea. They left for the North African country on 15 January 1895.

They stayed in the walled city of Blida, where the pair engaged in picking up attractive street boys and smoking the highly concentrated form of the marijuana plant, hashish. This blissful holiday would not last long without an explosive argument between Wilde and Bosie. Once again, Bosie stormed out saying he was going to take off with a local youth to the Algerian city of Biskra.

Left to his own devices and being far from home, Oscar over-indulged in risqué sexual liaisons with beautiful Algerian youths and smoking hashish. All this compromising behaviour was undertaken by Wilde in order to forget the constant campaign of harassment from Queensberry and his tempestuous relationship with Bosie. He returned from his Algerian indulgence on 31 January, leaving Bosie in Algeria. Constance was not back from Babbacombe, so Oscar decided, once again, not to reside at Tite Street but took rooms at the Hotel Avondale, located in London's Piccadilly.

Queensberry, having heard of Wilde's new play, acquired himself a ticket for the opening night. The marquess had form for interrupting performances he had an issue with. He had done this thirteen years previously at a performance of Lord Tennyson's play *The Promise of May*. Halfway through the performance, Queensberry – having taken issue with the fact that the villain was an agnostic – got up and interrupted the performance shouting: 'I am agnostic and I strongly protest against Mr Tennyson's gross caricature of our creed.' (http://aadl.org/node/539895)

It was Bosie's mother that alerted Wilde to her ex-husband's intentions. However, it was not because she liked Wilde, it was in order to protect her son's reputation. As mentioned previously, Wilde asked the theatre to write to Queensberry cancelling his ticket – claiming it had been sold twice by mistake. For extra peace of mind, Wilde also informed the local police that there may be trouble on opening night. The local police were happy to supply a visible presence at the St James's Theatre, to keep the peace. Constance had returned from Babbacombe, and although not totally well, managed to accompany her husband to his opening night at the St James's Theatre. The performance itself was a success, but Wilde later discovered he had been right to organise extra security for opening night. The Scarlet Marquess had still attempted to cause problems. He had arrived at the theatre accompanied by a ruffian and a grotesque boutique of vegetables for Wilde. He attempted to gain access to the theatre through various entrances and was eventually forced to leave his nasty gift for Wilde at the box office. Because this behaviour had been witnessed by the theatre staff, Wilde felt confident enough to approach his solicitors and instruct them to start the proceedings to prosecute Queensberry for his harassing behaviour. Sadly, Mr Humphery's was unable to do this, as none of the theatre staff were willing to give witness statements against Queensberry. Having heard of his father's behaviour, Bosie returned to London from Algeria and supported and encouraged Wilde to legally pursue his father.

It did not take long for Queensberry to make another attack on Wilde. On 28 February, Wilde went to the Albemarle Club. Due to how busy he had been with both *The Importance of Being Earnest*, and being away in Algeria, he had not visited his club in the best part of a month. Upon entering, the porter, Mr Wright, discreetly approached Wilde and told him a card had been left for him, ten days previously. He then gave Oscar an envelope and what he found inside would start a chain of events that would affect Wilde for the rest of his life.

Inside the envelope there was a calling card with the Marquess of Queensberry's details. On the reverse the marquess had scrawled: 'For Mr Oscar Wilde posing as somdomite [*sic*]'. Queensberry had gone into the club on the 18 February in order to embarrass Wilde and cause a scene. Discovering that Wilde was not there, Queensberry took one of his calling cards and wrote that insulting and misspelt message for Wilde. He did this right in front of the porter, Mr Wright, so that he could see what he had written. Wilde's first course of action was to return to the rooms at the Avondale and write a letter to Robbie Ross:

28 February 1895   Hotel Avondale, Piccadilly

Dearest Bobbie, Since I saw you something has happened. Bosie's father has left a card at my club with hideous words on it. I don't see anything now but criminal prosecution. My whole life seems ruined by this man. This tower of ivory is assailed by the foul thing. On the sand is my life split. I don't know what to do. If you could come here at 11.30 please do so tonight. I mar your life by trespassing ever on your love and kindness. I have asked Bosie to come tomorrow.

Ever Yours
Oscar

Unfortunately, Bosie was unable to wait until the following day and was there when Robbie Ross arrived at the Avondale. Long into that night the three friends discussed the best course of action to be taken.

The following morning, Wilde, Ross and Bosie went to see Oscar's solicitor, Mr Humphreys to seek his advice. With the evidence of the card, Humphreys Senior felt that Wilde had a good chance of prosecuting the marquess. During the course of their meeting, Oscar made one big mistake. When asked by his solicitor if there was any truth the allegations made by the Marquess of Queensberry, he lied, and said that there was no foundation whatsoever to the accusation. Had he been truthful at this time, he would have almost likely been advised that he could not win such a case and that his best course of action would be disassociate from Bosie and go into voluntary exile. Instead, Oscar chose to lie to his lawyer and follow the advice offered based on that lie. Wilde found that he went from being at the peak of his professional success, to a convicted prisoner in a matter of weeks.

Trials and Tribulations

'It's perfectly monstrous the way people
go about saying things against one, behind one's back,
that are absolutely not true.'

Oscar Wilde

After Oscar, Robbie Ross and Bosie visited Wilde's lawyers on 1 March. Mr Humphreys Senior applied for a warrant for Bosie's father to be arrested on the charges of libel. The following day, Saturday 2 March, at 9 am, the marquess was arrested at the Carter's Hotel in London, where he was staying. He was first taken to Vine Street police station to be questioned and then brought to Great Marlborough Street Magistrate court, where he was formally charged. The hearing at Great Marlborough Street Magistrate court was merely a formality. Mr Humphreys called the Albemarle Club porter, Mr Wright, to give a deposition describing what happened on 18 February:

> On 18 February last, the defendant came to the club and spoke to me. He handed me the card produced marked A, on which he had written in my presence 'for Oscar Wilde Ponce and Somdomite' ... he said 'Give this card to Oscar Wilde'. On the back of the card I wrote the time and date on which the card was handed to me. I put the card in the envelope marked B and addressed it to Oscar Wilde Esq.'
>
> *Irish Peacock & Scarlet Marquess,*
> Holland p.4

A second witness was brought forward by the defence team, this time it was the arresting officer, Mr Thomas Greet. He made a brief deposition as to what happened when Queensberry was arrested:

> About nine o'clock this morning I saw the defendant at Carter's Hotel, Albemarle Street. I said 'Are you the Marquess of Queensberry?' He said 'I am' I said 'I am a police officer and hold a warrant signed by R M Newton Esq of Marlborough Street police court for your arrest. I then read the warrant to him.
>
> *Irish peacock & Scarlet Marquess,*
> Holland p.5

The last part of his deposition is rather insightful in to Queensberry's level of dislike towards Wilde:

> {Queensberry}'What date?' I said 'The eighteenth' He said 'Yes – I have been trying to find Mr Oscar Wilde for eight or ten days. This thing has been going on for over two years'.
>
> *Irish Peacock & Scarlet Marquess,*
> Holland p.5

The hearing ended as an adjournment of a week was granted, bail granted to the marquess with a surety of sum of £1,500 – this was no small sum, the equivalent of around £123,000 today. The moneys were offered by William Tyser, a merchant, and Queensberry walked free.

A week later everyone once again attended the Great Marlborough Street Magistrate court. Further depositions were taken from Wilde and Queensberry. Oscar arrived at the magistrate's court accompanied by not just one, but two of the defendant's sons, Bosie and his brother, Percy Douglas. Wilde also maintained his flamboyant aesthetic style wearing a dark blue velvet trimmed overcoat adorned with a white flower in his button hole. During this relatively short hearing the magistrate and lawyers nitpicked at minor details in the witnesses' depositions and the magistrate ruled that there was indeed enough evidence for the marquess to be brought to criminal trial. This trial would be held at the Central Criminal Court, the Old Bailey. The same bail terms were requested. The case before the Central Criminal Court was to start on 3 April 1895.

Even during this short hearing, Wilde had to be told to answer questions precisely and factually. When asked 'Are you a dramatist and author?' Wilde gave a tongue-in-cheek response: 'I believe I am well-known as a dramatist and author'. He was reprimanded by the magistrate and so kept his answers to the point and factual.

Despite things going his way so far, Wilde was still worried about the possible outcomes. Several of his friends, including Frank Harris and Bernard Shaw, advised Wilde to drop the case and go abroad. They had made this seem like the best option and Wilde was coming around to this when Bosie joined the party and dismissed the idea of dropping the case – this, of course, would not have been in his selfish interest.

In the intervening weeks, all the evidence gathered by the marquess through his private detective, Cook, was dissected by his lawyers in order to build a case against Wilde. They needed to prove that he was in fact a homosexual, thereby proving that the words on the card could not be libel.

The case of Regina (on the prosecutions of Oscar Wilde) v John Douglas (Marquess of Queensberry) started on 3 April 1895 at the Old Bailey. The judge was Mr Justice Henn Collins. The courtroom was full of press and young lawyers wishing to witness legal history and public scandal first hand. The public gallery, though small, was also full to bursting with the general public. The ceremony and drama of court started as Queensberry took his place in the dock and then the twelve jurors were sworn in. The prosecuting side started by painting a positive picture of Wilde's life, background educational and professional successes and stressed the fact that he was married with two children and still resided at his family home.

Oscar was then called to the witness box and each point made in that opening statement was clarified and agreed by Wilde. Unlike his first appearance at the magistrate's court, this time he had opted for more sober attire, wearing a black morning coat, without his trademark floral buttonhole, and his tie was simply secured with a diamond and sapphire tie pin.

This first round of questions by his own lawyers did not seem to cause Oscar any grief. He answered the questions fully and even managed to get the courtroom to chuckle on several occasions. After about an hour it was time for the defence counsel to cross-examine him. Wilde had been classmates with Mr Edward Carson, and made a point of telling the court by saying that Carson would perform his role as with the bitterness of an old friend. The cross-questioning started badly when Carson pointed out that Wilde had been dishonest about his age, drawing the jurors' attention to the fact that Wilde had not been totally honest in his answers. This stretching the truth about his age was no doubt a habit he had picked up from his mother, Lady Wilde who was also often vague about her date of birth and age on forms and in conversation.

The cross examination did not get any better. The defence counsel started analysing Wilde's work, suggesting it was immoral and encouraged male readers to indulge in acts of gross indecency. At one point Carson drew comparisons between Wilde and one of his characters, Basil Hallward, the artist in the novel *The Picture of Dorian Gray*. After quoting a section of text from the novel Carson asked Wilde: 'have you ever had that experience towards a beautiful male person many years younger than yourself?' To which Wilde replied: 'I have given you my answer. Adoration is a thing I reserve for myself.' (*Irish Peacock & Scarlet Marquess*, Holland, pp.91–2)

Inevitably the questions started focusing on various young men known to Oscar. The defence lawyers, thanks to Queensberry's private detectives, were able to list names of young men who claimed to have had committed acts of gross indecency with Wilde. They were also able to including the dates and places that these acts were said to have taken place. Among those listed were Edward Shelley, Sidney Mavor, Fred Atkins, Maurice Schwabe, Alfred Wood, Charles Parker, Waiter Grainger and Alphonse Conway.

The questions were blunt, wanting to know how Oscar met these younger men, pointing out the big difference in age between them, commenting on their different social classes, as well as asking if he had given the youths cigarette cases, money or other gifts. Wilde soon recognised that he was in a very difficult and serious predicament. If these men were brought in as witnesses and questioned in depth, and in an open public courtroom, this could not only mean social ruin for him and Constance, but also could lead to criminal charges being brought. This would also give Queensberry the opportunity to hurt Wilde further and counter-sue him for having falsely accused him of libel. If he did drop the case and decide to go abroad this could be conceived as an admission of guilt by the press. Wilde must have felt so trapped.

Of course, due to the celebrity status of Wilde, the clandestine sexual nature of the case and Wilde's witty responses to many of the earlier questions, the press loved covering this case and it became the top headline for most of that day's and evening's papers.

The second day the questioning was even more direct when the defence counsel asked Wilde in what way he was intimate with these men many years younger than himself. The whole ordeal must have been humiliating. The defence, by raising the difference in social class between these younger men and Wilde was of course implying that these men indulged older men like Wilde in exchange for payment or gifts. At the end of the second day in court, Wilde returned to Holborn Viaduct Hotel where he was staying for the duration of the case. There, he and Bosie tried to find positives from the evidence already given.

The following morning Wilde's counsel, Sir Edward Clarke QC, arranged an early meeting at the court with Wilde, during which he was brutally frank. Clarke felt that due to the evidence already heard, the case was lost and that Queensberry would be acquitted. He strongly advised that Wilde withdraw his case. Sensibly, Wilde agreed. This also meant that he did not need to be present in the court again and he left the court discreetly by a backdoor. He returned to his quarters at the Holborn Viaduct Hotel and met with the Douglas brothers and Robbie Ross to try to work out what to do next.

In response to the press, Oscar wrote a letter to the *London Evening News* explaining that he had not wanted Bosie to take the stand, and that the Douglas family, with the exception of his father, were fully supportive of him. He also stressed that he had no intention of leaving London and intended to face any consequences that may arise from the last few days' events.

As expected, Queensberry left the court triumphant. And as expected, he was not going to let the matter rest with this victory. His solicitor spent that afternoon, writing to the head of the Crown Prosecutions Service ensuring that all of the incriminating evidence and trial transcripts were also added to the correspondence. Queensberry was taking no chances, he was out to ruin Wilde.

Still Wilde's friends tried to persuade him to go to France. Stubbornly, he refused. He then made his way to Cadogan Hotel, where Bosie had been staying for duration of the trial. On his way to the Cadogan, Oscar noticed that his name was no longer displayed outside either the St James's Theatre or the Haymarket. Both theatres had hoped that by disassociating the author's name with the play, that they could keep the plays running. It was not to be; the audience figures fell significantly both during and after the libel trial.

Oscar could not face Constance and sent Robbie Ross to tell her that the trial had failed. Like Ross, she thought Wilde should head to France and urged Ross to try to persuade her husband that it was the best option for. Bosie attempted to make himself useful and went to see his cousin, George Wyndham, at Westminster in order to try to get details of the prosecution against Oscar. This was would prove useless however. At 6.30 pm two plain clothed policemen knocked at the door of Bosie's hotel room. Wilde got up, put his coat on, picked up his gloves and a novel and went with the two police officers.

They first took him to Scotland Yard. Here he was read the full warrant and charges laid against him. Wilde's official charge was under section 11, of the 1885 Criminal Law Amendment Act, for committing acts of gross indecency with other male persons. From Scotland Yard he was brought to Bow Street Police Court. Here he was allotted a cell for the night. At ten o'clock the next morning Oscar was brought to the magistrate's court; when he was put into the the dock, he saw that Alfred

Taylor, his pimp, was also there. During this hearing with the magistrate, all the charges were presented and a list of witnesses announced. They were: the Parker brothers, Sidney, Mavor, Fred Atkins, Edward Shelley and Alfred Wood. If these men were willing to testify against Oscar, they would have been given immunity for subsequent charges against them in light of their evidence.

Poor Oscar had to listen to these men give detailed accounts of their intimate dealings with him. Sidney Mavor did in fact tell the court that they had met but that noting sexual had taken place between them. Given the number of witnesses needed to give depositions, this would not be a one day hearing and two further dates were booked to finish these accounts on the 11 and 19 of April. Again, Wilde was denied bail. As he had to wait longer than a night for his next hearing, he was relocated to Holloway prison. As he had not yet been convicted and was only on remand, the conditions at Holloway were far easier than those he would have to endure after his conviction. He could still wear his own clothes, he was able to pay for a furnished cell and was not obliged to eat the prison food but could have outside vittles brought to him. Other luxuries he was permitted included having visitors and access to books and writing materials, all of which were restricted or denied after he was convicted. During his time on remand, Wilde was visited daily by Bosie. After his conviction, however, Bosie never visited him. Robbie Ross had been advised to go to France as he had been summoned to give evidence against Oscar.

After the two further hearings in front of the magistrate, it was ruled that there was enough evidence to go to Criminal Crown Court. Wilde's trial was booked for 26 April 1895, just a week after it had been committed to crown court by the magistrate.

As Wilde started to plan his defence with his lawyers, Constance had left Tite Street. Merchants and tradesmen were demanding long overdue payments. On 24 April there was an official auction at their home, where the remaining items in the Wildes' household were sold off in order to settle the accrued debts. Everything went under the hammer, clothes, books, art, household items and even Cyril and Vyvyan's toys. The money made at the sale did not even cover the outstanding debts.

Two days after that auction, on 26 April 1895, Oscar's trial started. In all, there were twenty-five counts of gross indecency to be tried. Each of the witnesses were questioned in order to get the most graphic details of their time spent with Wilde. It took several days to hear all their testimonies and for them to be cross-examined by the defence. Other evidence presented against Wilde included the transcript of the failed libel case against Queensberry.

On 30 April, it was Oscar's turn to be cross-examined in the dock. At no point did Wilde deny knowing any of the men called as witnesses against him, but he did deny the allegation of any acts of gross indecency with each witness. This cross-examination took the full day.

The next day, 1 May, the judge summed up the evidence and the two counsels gave their closing speeches to the court and jury. The jury left the court to deliberate at 1.30 pm. They stopped for lunch at 3 pm and returned to the courtroom at 5.15 pm, where they told the court that they had failed to reach a verdict. As a result of it being a hung jury, Oscar was sent back to Holloway. His counsel applied for bail, which was be granted on 3 May, but the amount it was set at was a huge sum of £5,000 (an estimated £410,246 today). It is not surprising that it took several days for the full amount to be found and borrowed. Oscar was released from Holloway on 7 May 1895.

Bosie, meanwhile, had been persuaded to go to France ahead of Oscar's trial and was still there when Wilde was released on bail on 7 May. Upon being granted his freedom Oscar met up with his counsel at the Midland Hotel, attached to St Pancreas station in London. Through ill luck or fate, while Wilde was there, Queensberry arrived at the hotel. Even though he could not see Bosie as he was still in France, the Marquess, convinced Bosie was aiding and supporting Wilde, followed him and his legal team when they decided to relocate up the road to The Great Northern Hotel, attached to neighbouring Kings Cross Station.

That evening Oscar sought sanctuary with his older brother Willie and his new wife at Oakley Street. Lady Wilde was also living with Willie at this time. Begrudgingly, Willie allowed his brother room on a camp bed. For many of those days at Oakley Street, between his trials, Oscar drunk himself into a stupor. Thankfully, his good friend Ada Leverson and her husband rescued him from Willie and brought him to stay with them until he went to retrial on the 20 May.

Oscar's retrial with Taylor was set to start on 20 May at the Old Bailey. His solicitor, Mr Humphreys was also able to get Wilde's case to be heard separately from Alfred Taylor. This was in the hope that the trial would be less biased against Wilde. It also meant that Wilde was now only facing eight charges of gross indecency, rather than twenty-five with Taylor. The judge hearing the case was one of Wilde's neighbours from Tite Street, Mr Justice Wills. As Taylor and Wilde were now to be tried separately, the start of his retrial was delayed by a day.

As if Oscar was not already in a highly stressful situation, Queensberry once again managed to make things worse for him. On the same day the retrial commenced, Queensberry issued a demand for costs to the sum of £677 (approximately £55,550 in today's money). Wilde had seven days to pay the bill or he will be declared bankrupt. This poor timing would not helped Oscar's morale.

After a new jury was sworn in, the retrial of began. Because it was a retrial no new evidence was introduced and so press interest decreased. There would be no news story until the verdict was reached. The final day of the trial was Saturday 25 May 1895. The closing arguments and statements were made and the jury retired to deliberate at 3.30 pm. Wilde was made to wait in the holding cells below the courtroom for the verdict. The jury enquired about a piece of evidence around 5.30 pm; shortly after, they were able to reach a verdict and return to the courtroom. Wilde had been found guilty of seven of the eight charges laid against him. Justice Willis then sentenced Wilde to two years' imprisonment with hard labour. Life was about to get much harder for Oscar Wilde.

PRISONER C33

'It is not the prisoners who need
reformation, it is the prisons.'

Oscar Wilde

While touring the United States in 1882, Oscar Wilde had visited a prison and had felt compassion for the men he saw behind bars. When touring their cells he even found copies of literature. However, this would not be the reality of Wilde's experience of prison; it was far from what he had romanticised about after visiting the US prison. In many respects, Wilde was lucky to survive his prison experience at all.

The British Victorian prison system involved, as one expects, a truly harsh daily routine; it also separated the incarcerated, no interaction was allowed. This was so the prisoners could reflect upon their crimes and understand why they were being punished. This was further reinforced by compulsory attendance of chapel each Sunday, where once again, interaction between inmates was strictly prohibited.

Oscar Wilde was found guilty of gross indecency and sentenced on Saturday 25 May 1895. Because he was sentenced on a Saturday he would have to send the first two nights of his sentence in Newgate prison, in Central London. This was prior to being transferred to the first of three prisons in which he would serve his sentence of hard labour over the next two years.

Prisoners like Oscar, sentenced to hard labour, were expected to reach certain daily gaols to earn their evening meal. Prisoners had to walk 8,640 feet on a vertical treadmill attached to the wall. That around 2.6 Kilometres or 1.6 miles. Alternatively, some inmates had to turn a crank 10,000 times in a day. If the boredom did not affect the the prisoner, then the repetition of the exercise on their joints would add to the misery they were already suffering. If the wardens who oversaw these activities thought that any prisoner was finding the tasks too easy, they would tighten bolts to make the task harder to perform.

These high impact labours were undertaken and performed by men who were generally not in the best physical health due to poverty prior to their conviction. In contrast, modern athletes who put their bodies through rigorous, hard physical activity not only train sensibly and gradually, but take rest days and refrain from training when they are either injured or ill. They also have a balanced and nutritious diet.

The 'food' provided by the prison was barely enough to keep a man alive. The prisoners' diet was made up of a thin gruel; gruel being a watery slop made up of water and the bare minimum amount of oats boiled to a slightly thick consistency. Some gruel also had offal, grizzle or lard added, though they were not fresh, nor was there enough to give the gruel taste, or be better for the men nutritionally. This would be served with water and stale bread. These prisoners were expected to perform their tasks on next to no calories. Not only was this diet bland and tasteless, it was often unfit for human consumption and frequently made the men sick. Dysentery and cholera were common in the prison due to poor food and lack of hygiene when the prisoners were ill. On top of all this, the lack of vitamins, nutrients and minerals also led to conditions such as scurvy. The lack of interaction and deliberate isolation the prisoners were forced to live under would also have harmful consequence for their mental wellbeing. These were the conditions that Oscar Wilde walked into in 1895 – nothing short of a living hell.

On Monday 27 May, Wilde was transferred by van to Pentonville prison in North London. His welcome to prison life was humiliating and cruel. Wilde was by no means given special treatment due to his status of being a well-known individual – if anything this made him a target for the less scrupulous wardens. After attending to the administration, the warders shaved the heads of all new inmates. For Oscar Wilde the aesthete, known for his well-groomed long locks, this must have been a deeper humiliation than for other inmates. After his hair was badly shaven off, he was made to strip off all his clothes, was weighed and then made to get in to a filthy bath with used dirty water from previous inductees. In Oscar's case he would have come out dirtier than when he went in. It is little wonder that in his last years he enjoyed spending money he did not have on perfumes and colognes.

Once washed and dried, he was given his prison uniform: a coarse, rough suit of clothes with the distinctive motif of arrows. This was so that the prisoners could be recognised should the manage the near impossible – to escape the prison. Next, like all new inmates, Wilde was subjected to a 'medical' examination. This had nothing to do with the wellbeing of the prisoner, but to determine what kind of hard labour the inmate should undertake. The last part of this welcome was to be given a draft of potassium bromide. This was used as a sedative to help the new prisoners acclimatise to their changed circumstances. There were, however, some nasty side effects – both physically and mentally – to the potassium bromide. For the majority of prisoners, the potassium increased a depressive state, and this was in addition to the nausea and vomiting it cased in most prisoners.

Oscar would next have been brought to his cell. The Victorians had redeveloped their new prisons to have poorly ventilated cells designed for single occupancy. Given the illness and disease rampant in these gaols, the smell for both inmates and staff must have been little better than open sewers most of the time. To add to the gloomy atmosphere, the small cells were poorly lit, and roughly measured 13 ft long and 7 ft wide. Within this small space, there was a hard plank bed, small table and chamber pot. The chamber pot was to be emptied by the prisoner several times a day but only at scheduled times. If it was full, it was full. No wonder dysentery, and cholera were rampant within the prisons.

Wilde's physical and mental health deteriorated rapidly. He too contracted stomach issues causing violent and continuous bouts of diarrhoea. He then started to refuse to eat the 'food' that he was given, claiming that it was the source of his illness. In turn, this weakened Wilde further physically. From his schooldays, Oscar had always been a solidly built, tall man, and quickly he started to waste away. He worried the authorities so much that he was sent to the prison's infirmary were he was treated and re-evaluated. As a result, Wilde's was recategorised as a second-class hard labour inmate. This meant that once out of the sickbay, he was made to pick oakum as his punishment. This was a repetitive task consisting of separating the fibres of old rope by hand. The prisoners were given no tools to help them do this and much of the rope was coated in substances such as tar, making the process even harder. Fingers and hands would become sore, calloused and infected. Picking oakum was also an activity the poor of the Victorian workhouses had to undertake for their bed and board.

For the first three months of their imprisonment, prisoners were not allowed any reading material other than the Bible, and after that time would be granted access to the library. It is worth noting that the majority of poor men at this time were barely literate, so this was not a perk that all could enjoy. The contents of the library were uninspiring and made up of poor quality religious tracts intended to make the prisoners reflect upon their sins, crimes and life. One of the hardest things Wilde found about prison was the lack of access to reading and writing materials although, this did improve when he was reallocated later in his prison sentence.

In 1895, the then serving Home Secretary (and future the Prime Minister) was Herbert Asquith. Asquith and Wilde were known to each other socially, they were both members of the Albemarle Club. Wilde was also good friends with Asquith's wife, Margot, whom he had met at a garden party in late 1880, prior to her marriage to Asquith. Wilde even dedicated one of his short stories to Margot – *The Star Child*. Sadly Margot, who in fairness was in a very difficult position, would not support her friend in 1895 during the scandal, subsequent trials and later imprisonment. However, her husband was able to use his position as Home Secretary to visit Wilde.

Since his incarceration, there had been an increasing number of stories in the British press concerning his physical and mental health, as well as his wellbeing. On 5 June, Asquith enquired with the prison hospital and doctor to the status of Wilde's health. The response was that he was well mentally and physically and was not causing any worry to the staff regarding his general health. This, of course, was far from the truth. Thankfully, another of Wilde's social connections and friends decided to be more thorough in investigating the wellbeing of their fallen friend.

Richard Haldane was a Scottish Liberal and later Labour MP, and like Asquith, was known to Wilde socially during the height of his success. Prior to following a political career, Haldane had qualified as barrister. He decided to stand for the 1885 November election and won his seat for Haddingtonshire (now East Lothian). He would go on to hold his seat until 1911.

In 1894, he formed part of the Gladstone Committee, whose job it was to look at the treatment of younger prisoners aged 16–21. The committee felt that these prisoners should be educated and industrially trained in order to set them up for success after their release. They were not, therefore, to be subjected to the harsher routines endured by older prisoners. Thanks to being part of this government committee, Haldane had the legal authority to enter prisons. Using this special access, he took it upon himself to visit his friend Wilde in prison, in order to see how he was doing for himself. The man he saw was a broken and diminished form of the man Haldane had previously known. This visit would mean a lot to Oscar, and he would dedicate *The Ballad of Reading Gaol* to Haldane. Haldane was also instrumental in getting proper reading materials to his friend.

This visit was the catalyst for the first of two prison transfers during Wilde's sentence. On 4 July, he was moved from Pentonville to Wandsworth prison. The exact reasoning is not clear, however there was a chaplain at Wandsworth by the name Rev. William Douglas Morrison, whose writings on the prison system were a catalyst for the formation of the Gladstone committee. Haldane may have hoped that the chaplain could help and comfort Wilde and unofficially keep an eye on his wellbeing. The reality was that Wilde found Wandsworth far harder than Pentonville had been. In Frank Harris's biography *Oscar Wilde, His Life & Confessions* (chapter 17), Oscar is quoted as saying: 'Wandsworth is the worst. No dungeon in hell could be worse.' He later confessed that he hoped he would die during his time in Wandsworth because it was that bad.

While Wilde was in prison, he had been declared bankrupt due the Marquess of Queensberry suing him for the heavy legal costs from the libel case. This would have been another personal setback and misfortune that would have affected his morale and mental wellbeing. Wilde also learnt that Bosie was planning to publish a personal defence of Wilde entitled 'On the case of Mr Oscar Wilde' in the French journal, *Mercure de France*. This defence would have quoted large extracts of their personal correspondence, hoping to prove that their relationship had been noble. Wilde asked his friend Robert Harborough Sherard to write to the editor of the publication in France. The publication in turn wrote to Bosie asking that he write the piece, but without the inclusion of the personal letters between himself and Wilde. In a trademark immature rage, Bosie responded that they either publish it as it was or not at all. The piece was never published.

The personal consequences for Oscar, had the defence been published, would have been painful as he and Constance had agreed to postpone starting divorce proceedings. This was decided after Constance visited her husband in Wandsworth prison during September 1895. It was also during this visit, that Oscar profusely apologised to Constance and begged forgiveness for his behaviour over the previous three years. This would have been an emotionally difficult visit for both parties and it is testament to their friendship, respect and love for each other. Although they may not have been romantically or sexually in love with each other at this point, Constance and Wilde did love each other as friends, and as the parents to their sons. Given Constance's wiliness to listen and forgive her husband, she may still have had held an affectionate love for him.

It would be while Oscar was in Wandsworth that he would damage his ear badly. This injury would eventually be the cause of his final illness and play a part in his subsequent death in 1900. On the first Sunday of October 1895, Wilde was struggling to get out of bed. The prison doctor saw him but accused him of avoiding chapel and being a malingerer. After threats of even worse punishment, Wilde managed to get up and go to the chapel but was unable to stand and kept falling over. It was during one of these falls that he hit his head, damaged his ear and lost consciousness. Later, Oscar regained consciousness in a hospital cell and would remain in the hospital – later on the ward, until he was transferred for the second and final time to Reading Gaol. This took place in the last week of November 1895.

After his fall, a new inquiry into Wilde's state of health, both physical and mental, was requested by the Asquith's Home Office. The two men in charge of this investigation were David Nicholson, who was a medical superintendent at Broadmoor, and Richard Brayn, governor and medical officer for female convicts in Woking prison. They met and examined Oscar on 22 October 1895, reporting back that he was sane with no sign of derangement and that physically he was 'satisfactory'. Given that he was receiving medical care in the infirmary, rather than under regular prison routine, this was neither a fair or accurate report. They also said that he had not been mistreated and that any depression was due to his nature, not his treatment within the prison. However, they did recommend that Wilde be transferred to a prison outside of the capital and located in the countryside, as he would be well suited to outside exercise and fresh air. They also suggested that any employment set for Oscar should be varied and be more in line with activities such as bookbinding or gardening, rather than picking oakum. It was also recommended Oscar was given a wider range of reading materials.

No blame was directed at the cruel, bullying guards and wardens, or the inhumane way they treated all prisoners. By relocating Wilde they were taking him away from the scrutiny of the press in London, rather than for his wellbeing. It also meant that there could be a more relaxed approach to his punishment. This was thought to be the best outcome for both parties, given the circumstances.

Wandsworth had one more humiliation in store for Wilde before Reading took over his care; the transfer itself was unnecessarily cruel and caused Oscar great trauma. On 20 November, instead of transferring him in a prison cart or van, the guards took Oscar – handcuffed and still in prison uniform – to the nearest train station, Clapham Junction. Here, he was made to wait in the cold and rain, in full view of other travellers on the platform, for half an hour. During this time he was jeered at, laughed at, verbally insulted, spat at and stared at by his fellow commuters.

Once safely in Reading Gaol, the governor, Lieutenant Colonel Henry Isaacson, saw how traumatised Oscar was following this humiliation. When Wilde said he did not want change prison again and wanted to serve the rest of his sentence in Reading, he was reassured he would not be subjected to that experience again.

Just prior to his transfer Wilde had endured another humiliation when he had to go through his expenses and spending with the bankruptcy receiver. He was made to explain every expense. He had spent £5,000 (about £460,000 today) on Bosie alone. This must have made him feel so guilty, given that he was always struggling to pay basic household bills for his family. It was as a result of this meeting that Constance and the boys had to watch their household being auctioned off to pay Oscar's debts – the biggest being the legal costs claimed by Queensberry.

In early December 1895, Wilde learnt that Constance and the boys had legally changed their surname to Holland; this too would have been emotional blow for Wilde. From 1895 until his death in 1900, Wilde repeatedly asked his friends about the welfare of his boys. If nothing else, he loved them greatly and knowing that he would likely never see them again was by far the worst punishment to him psychologically.

The injury to his ear had little improved despite his time in Wandsworth infirmary prior to relocation to Reading. Weeks on, it was still frequently bleeding, oozing fluid and pus. And despite the recommendations by Nicholson and Brayn, Wilde was still made to do his quota of labour, including the monotonous picking of oakum. Lieutenant Colonel Henry Isaacson, would also punish him for minor misdemeanours by withholding his books.

During February 1896, Constance, who was then in northern Italy, made the journey back to England and to Reading Gaol to break the news to Oscar, that his beloved mother had died. Oscar recalled this meeting with Constance in a letter to Robbie Ross of 1 April 1897: 'Her sweetness in coming here from Italy to break to me the news of my mother's death.' During this meeting with his estranged wife, Constance also talked of the future of their marriage and their boys. Little did either of them know that this would be the last time that they would meet each other in person.

In May 1896, just after the halfway point in his sentence, Oscar received a visit from Robert Ross and Robert Harborough Sherard. During this visit the friends were horrified at the deteriorated state of Oscar's physical and mental health. Oscar spent most of their visit crying. He instructed Ross and Sherard to get Bosie to surrender all letters and gifts he had sent him. Sherard noted that Oscar was in an even worse state than when he had seen him in Wandsworth.

After their visit, Ross and Sherard met with more of their friends. Among these mutual friends was Frank Harris. All who met tried to work out how they could find a way to get Oscar's conditions improved, as they all feared if things did not improve, Oscar would die before his sentence ended. It was decided that Harris would meet the newly appointed Chairman of the Prison Commissioner, Evelyn Ruggles-Brise. Ruggles-Brise was willing to listen to Harris's concerns and sent him to Reading to assess Wilde for himself and report back. Frank Harris met his friend Oscar on 16 June 1896. During their meeting Harris reassured Wilde that he would try to get his books and some writing materials restored to him, as well as try to improve his conditions. Harris also met with Lieutenant Colonel Isaacson on 16 June. Isaacson would openly boast with a swagger that he and the prison doctor were 'knocking the nonsense out of Wilde' (Hyde, *Oscar Wilde: The Aftermath*, p.64). No doubt Oscar was persecuted like this on purpose; due to the nature of his conviction, these men saw it as their duty to make Wilde a 'real man', while under their charge.

Thankfully, after Frank Harris reported back to Evelyn Ruggles-Brise, changes did happen, though they were not immediate. First, Oscar wrote to the Home Secretary petitioning for early release. In the letter he claimed that his homosexual tendencies were a form of madness requiring medical help rather than harsh punishment. He went on to explain how he was an intellectual and needed brain stimulation in reading materials to survive. He also criticised the medical care he had received at Reading. Lieutenant Colonel Isaacson did pass this on unaltered, but included a new medical report to be considered, alongside Wilde's petition. The report stated that Wilde's health, both physically and mentally, had improved since he had arrived at Reading.

This letter to the Home Office prompted another inspection of Reading, focusing on their treatment of Wilde. These results were finally presented to Ruggles-Brise on 10 July. Again, the report stated that Wilde was being treated well but that there should be a more detailed examination of his eyesight (Wilde had said his sight had been ruined through working and reading in his poorly lit cell) and of his hearing. The further medical examinations into his sight and hearing never took place, but other measures in the report did happen. Again, it was agreed that Wilde should have access to more books as well as have access to writing materials.

No long after the report, Lieutenant Colonel Isaacson was replaced as governor of Reading Gaol. The new governor was a far gentler man, Major James O. Nelson. Wilde submitted a list of books and reading materials that he would like to have; this included: a Greek testament, Milman's *History of the Jews*, Farrar's *St Paul*, Dante's *Divine Comedy*, Renan's *Vie de Jesus* in French, poetry by Tennyson, Keats, Chaucer and Marlowe. Major Nelson approved the list with no issue. The relationship between Wilde and the new prison governor was far more positive. Nelson later described his former inmate as 'A gentle man and humane character greatly liked and respected by all the prisoners'. He also described Wilde privately as 'the most Christ-like man I ever met.' (Frankel, *Oscar Wilde the Unrepentant Years* p.61)

One of the most inescapable truths during this time in Wilde's life, is that Bosie – the cause of all Wilde's downfalls – never once visited or even wrote to his former lover and friend during his incarceration.

The new privilege of being allowed writing materials in his free time, would allow Oscar to write one of his last two pieces of work. It was the letter that Oscar composed to Bosie that would later be published under the name *De Profundis*, which translates as 'from the depths' and it is taken from the Old Testament, Psalm 130, and is a very apt name for the piece. Oscar began writing it in January 1897, and completed the 50,000-word letter that March. It had been at the suggestion of the new governor, Major Neilson, who had encouraged Oscar to write his thoughts and reflections down – *De Profundis* was the result. After Wilde had completed each page, he was not allowed to correct it, instead it was taken and kept safe. Once the piece was complete, he could reread and correct the full letter. Then it was kept by Neilsen until Oscar's release, when the governor gave the letter to him as he left Reading.

The letter is made up of two parts, the first is a reflection upon the relationship between Wilde and Bosie. Here, Oscar reiterates the hard truths and virulent and destructive nature of their relationship. Wilde himself says it best: 'I don't write this letter to put bitterness into your heart, but to pluck it out of mine.' The second part of the letter is a far deeper personal reflection on Wilde's religious and spiritual journey in prison. In this part of the letter, Wilde draws similarities to himself and Christ – it was a Christ that has been given the Wildean flare and overly romanticised: 'I see a far more intimate and immediate connection between the true life of Christ and the true life of the artist.'

The writing of *De Profundis* reveals much about the *real* Oscar Wilde, the man he was, his sense of humanity, his understanding of emotions, his intellect, his growth as a man and life in general. Of all his work this is the work that shows the reader the true Oscar Wilde, raw and flawed.

Also during the last days of his prison sentence, Oscar learned of three small children who had been brought in after being caught stealing rabbits. Despite his own personal woes, and bankruptcy, Wilde decided to help the children get released. In order to find out why these three children were in prison, Oscar wrote to one of the guards, Warder Martin, in order to find how they came to be locked up.

17 May 1897   Reading Prison

Please find out the Name of A.2.11 Also the names of the children who are in for the rabbits and the amount of the fine. Can I pay this, and get them out? If so I will get them out tomorrow. Please dear friend, do this for me. I must get them out. Think what a thing for me it would be to be able to help three little children. I would be delighted beyond words. If I can do this by paying the fine, tell the children that they are to be released tomorrow by a friend, and ask them to be happy and not to tell anyone.

As Wilde's sentence was drawing to a close, the Berkshire town of Reading was starting to fill up with the press from as far away as the United States. Major Neilsen had been offered money for some of the American press to have access to Oscar for an interview, on the morning of his release. It was therefore thought wise to find a less public way for Wilde to walk to his liberation. Two days prior to his release, on 17 May 1897, Wilde was informed that he would be transferred back to Pentonville for the last night of his sentence and released early on the morning of 19 May. He was also assured that he would not suffer the cruel humiliation he had during his move from Wandsworth to Reading.

On the evening of 18 May 1897, Oscar, dressed in conservative civilian clothes and unshackled, left HMP Reading and was escorted by the Deputy Governor, Warder Harrison. They were transported to the quiet Berkshire station of Taplow rather than the busy station at Reading. Here they boarded an express train towards London Paddington. The journey and deception went off without a flaw. Harrison and Wilde left the train at Westbourne Park and took a public taxi to Pentonville Prison. This had been where his imprisonment had started two years previously. The following morning, at 6.15, Oscar walked through the door of Pentonville prison to his freedom and his awaiting friends. Freedom for Oscar would also come with its fair share of hardships.

SEBASTIAN
MELMOTH IN EXILE

'Everyone is born a king;
some people die in exile.'

Oscar Wilde

When Oscar Wilde walked to his liberty through the door of Pentonville prison at 6.15 am on 19 May 1897, he was met by his friends More Adey and Stewart Headlam, who collected him in curtained carriage that they had been permitted to bring into the prison forecourt behind the gates. As the press were unaware of Wilde's relocation to Pentonville, this ride to freedom was thankfully problem free.

The friends brought Oscar back to Stewart Headlam's Bloomsbury abode. The interior of which would have raised Wilde's spirits further, for it was decorated with Morris and Company Wallpapers and had Pre-Raphaelite pictures upon the walls. The first thing that Oscar did was make use of Headlam's bathroom facilities where he washed the last traces of prison life from his person and put on some new clothes. Then he had his first cup of coffee in two years.

That morning Oscar's friends the Leversons and the Cliftons came to celebrate his release. Much to their relief, when Oscar went to see his friends he entered the room cigarette in hand, a flower in his buttonhole and full of his usual banter and wit. Ada Leverson, upon whom Wilde had bestowed the moniker of 'Sphinx', felt that Oscar's time at Her Majesty's pleasure, had made him 'Slighter and younger'.

There were discussions about Wilde's future. Robbie Ross and Reggie Turner had already travelled to Dieppe and were waiting his arrival. But due to the excitement of being reunited with some of his favourite friends, the planned morning train and boat from Newhaven to Normandy was missed. Instead, Wilde and More Adey, with whom he was travelling, took to the night train and boat instead. Wilde telegrammed Ross of the change of plan.

> 19 May 6.25pm
>
> Arriving by night Boat. Am so delighted at the prospect of seeing you and Reggie ... More has been such a good friend to me and I am grateful to you all I cannot find the words to express my feelings. You must not dream of waiting up for us. In the morning we will meet. Please engage rooms for us at your hotel. When I see you I shall be quite happy, indeed I am happy now to think I have such wonderful friendship shown to me.
>
> Sebastian Melmoth

It had been decided that Oscar should utilise a different identity when travelling, at least for the first few years after his release. The name chosen for Wilde's travelling name was Sebastian Melmoth. Sebastian was inspired by the beautiful Renaissance art depictions of the tragic martyred saint that Wilde loved – St Sebastian. While Melmoth was inspired the main character in the Charles Robert Maturin novel, *Melmoth the Wanderer*. Given how much Wilde moved around in the next two-and-half years as he struggled to settle into life after prison, the name Melmoth was somewhat apt.

The night boat arrived in Normandy at 4.00 am and both Robbie Ross and Reggie Turner were waiting on the dockside to greet Wilde. Robbie in particular could see a big difference from the man that he had visited in Reading Gaol. Oscar's face had lost its coarseness, and seemed to have gained a youthful appearance. It was also at this reunion on the quayside that Wilde gave Robbie the big envelope containing his long letter to Bosie, which would be published posthumously as *De Profundis*.

Turner and Ross had been busy setting things up for their friend. They had booked rooms for him at Hotel Sandwich, a small discreet hotel in Dieppe, located on Rue de la Halle au Blé. The friends had organised a little celebration, complete with wine and sandwiches. This seemed to have momentarily overwhelmed Oscar who broke down and cried at their kindness.

The thoughtfulness of Oscar's friends did not end with the little celebration as they had placed flowers and a selection of books for him to read in his rooms. There were also an assortment of letters waiting for him from friends that he had not been able to see the day before. Among the letters was a gift of £50 and two new suits from his friend and later biographer, Frank Harris. Ross and Turner would stay with Oscar helping him acclimatise to his new freedom for a week before returning to England.

During the first few days of freedom, Wilde learnt from an article in the *Daily Chronicle* that one of his wardens, Warden Martin had been dismissed from his job at Reading Gaol. He was dismissed as he had been reported for giving a biscuit to one of the small children convicted of stealing rabbits. Wilde, who had helped get the small children released, was outraged that this kindness to a small child, this act of humanity and compassion, was seen as wrong and was punished in such a manner. He wrote to the editor of the *Daily Chronicle*, giving a heartfelt defence of Warden Martin's actions as well as a taste of the realities of being imprisoned:

27 May 1897   Dieppe

Sir, I learn with regret, through the columns of your paper, that the warder Martin, of Reading Prison has been dismissed by the Prison Commissioners for having given some sweet biscuits to a little hungry child. I saw the three children myself on the Monday preceding my release ... They were quite small children, the youngest – the one to whom the warder gave the biscuits – being a tiny little chap, for whom they had evidently been unable to find clothes small enough to fit. I had of course, seen many children in prison during the two years ... but the little child I saw on the afternoon of Monday 17 May, at Reading was tinier than any of them.

Both Ross and Turner tried and failed to dissuade Wilde from making such a public statement, fearing it would help neither his rehabilitation nor reputation. Having seen the eloquent and passionate extracts above, in this instance their concerns were thankfully misplaced.

The letter continues:

> The present treatment of children is terrible, primarily from the people not understanding the peculiar psychology of a child's nature. A child can understand a punishment inflicted by an individual, such as parent or guardian, and bear it with a certain amount of acquiescence. What it cannot understand is a punishment inflicted by society.

The letter to the editor is many pages long and is an insightful, intelligent, empathic and humane essay concerning Wilde's thoughts on children within the Victorian prison system. This letter to the *Chronicle* is far more representative of the real Oscar Wilde than any of his plays or other writings.

After two years with no access to the finer things in life, it is little wonder, that upon his release and with access to money again, that Wilde fell into old habits of over-generosity and over-spending. He was particularly fond of spending money at the local *marché* in Dieppe and was often spotted near the stall selling perfumes and oils. Again, after two years in several prisons, which stank due to the poor food and prisoners' poor hygiene and constant sickness, it was little wonder that he found solace in the small pleasures, such as perfume and cologne.

As tourist season encroached upon Normandy, it was thought wiser for 'Sebastian Melmoth' to relocate to the nearby small village of Berneval-sur-Mer, and stay in another discreet hotel, the Hôtel de la Plage. Unfortunately, Berneval-sur-Mer was not as busy as Dieppe had been, and once again Oscar found himself isolated and lonely in his new life. Thankfully, he turned his mind to writing letters as a way to keep in touch with his friends and ease his loneliness. Despite Robbie Ross leaving only the day before, Wilde composes a long letter to him on 28 May 1897:

> My Dear Robbie, this is my first day alone, and of course a very unhappy one. I begin to realise my terrible position of isolation, and I have been rebellious and bitter of heart all day. Is it not sad? I thought I was accepting everything so well and simply, and I have had moods of rage … Bosies revolting letter was in the room, and foolishly I had read it again and left it by my bedside …I feel him as an evil influence, poor fellow. To be with him would be to return to hell from which I do think I have been released. I Hope to never see him again.

Another correspondent of Wilde's was his former governor at Reading Prison, Major Nelson. Nelson had made the last months of Wilde's incarceration more humane and compassionate;

> 28 May 1897   Hôtel de la plage, Berneval-sur-Mer
>
> Dear Major Nelson
> I had of course intended to write to you as soon as I had safely reached French soil, to express, however inadequately, my real feelings of what you must let me term, not merely sincere, but affectionate gratitude to you for your kindness and gentleness to me in prison, and for the real care that you took of me at the end when I was mentally upset and in a terrible nervous excitement.

He continues his letter to Major Nelson in a reflective, compassionate mood:

> I abstained from writing, however, because I was haunted by the memory of the little children, and the wretched

half-witted lad who was flogged by the doctor's orders. I could not have kept them out of my letter, and to have mentioned them to you might have put you in a difficult position. ... I longed to speak to you about these things on the evening of my departure but I felt that in my position as a prisoner it would have been wrong of me to do so, and that it would, or might, have put you in a difficult position.

It was not just maintaining friendships via mail that eased Oscar's loneliness, he also met local people, one of which was the Catholic priest with whom he enjoyed discussing religion and stained glass.

At this turning point in his new life, it was not surprising that Oscar sought to reconnect with his estranged wife Constance, who was also on the European mainland at this time with their boys, Cyril and Vyvyan. The boys were boarding at their respective schools in Germany and in the south of France. Oscar was desperate to see his sons, as well as trying and reconcile with Constance. Although there are no records of his letters to Constance, there is correspondence between Wilde and the couple's mutual friend Carlos Blacker, in which he alludes to his correspondence with her. On Thursday 29 July 1897, just over two months since his release from prison, Oscar wrote to Blacker:

Thursday 29 July 1897   Cafe Sussie Dieppe

Dear Friend, I am terribly distressed about what you tell me about Constance. I had no idea it was so serious. Of course she could not come here. I see that .... and the journey would be too much.

[...]

I am so glad she is with you and your charming, brilliant wife. For myself, I really am quite heart-broken.

On 4 August Wilde again writes to Blacker and responds to a letter that seems to have been received since his last. In this letter, Oscar seems to have accepted that it is not a good thing for him to travel to Genoa to see Constance at this time, while she is so unwell:

> My Dear Friend, I am simply heart broken at what you tell me. I don't mind *my life* being wrecked – that is as it should be – but when I think of poor Constance I simply want to kill myself. But I suppose I must live through it all. ... Of course I think it would be much better for Constance to see me, but you think not. Well you are wiser.

Oscar must have thought that any possibility of resuming, even a fraction of the family life he had shared with Constance and the boys up until 1895, was no longer an option. And in that sadness and distress, Oscar thought of one person with whom he had felt adored and loved – Lord Alfred 'Bosie' Douglas, who had also been the cause of all his problems since they had met in 1891.

Despite Wilde writing to Robbie Ross on 28 May 1897, stating that he 'Hopes never to see him [Bosie] again', by the 2 June – less than a week later – Oscar had replied to the letter from Bosie which he had previously described as 'revolting'. The letter, unlike *De Profundis*, was once again loving and flattering, so much so it could have been written in the weeks prior to his arrest and trials. It is as if nothing had gone wrong; Oscar was finding comfort in the places he had found it before. He starts the letter with 'My dear Boy' – not exactly the way one would address someone you never want to see again: 'Always write to me about your art and the art of others. It is better to meet on the double peak of Parnassus than elsewhere. I have read your poems with great pleasure and interest.'

Indeed, this letter writing to Bosie continued at first daily then at least weekly, and the pair started to plan for Bosie to come to Normandy to visit Oscar. This plan did not go smoothly. First, there seems to have been issues with the post, letters taking two days to arrive or getting lost.

> I found a letter from you dated 11 June (that is last Friday) but posted on 13 June (Last Sunday) … You asked me in it to let you come on Saturday: but, dear honey-sweet boy I have already asked you to come then so we both have the same desire as usual. Your name is to be Jonquil du Vallon.

These carefully laid out plans for Bosie to travel to Normandy and stay with Oscar would have to put on pause as Wilde received a letter from his solicitor informing him that Queensberry was aware of their plans. He subsequently writes to Bosie:

Thursday 17 June 1897   Cafe Suisse Dieppe

> My dearest boy I have been obliged to ask my friends to leave me, as I am so upset and distressed in nerve by my solicitor's letter and the apprehension of serious danger …. Of course at present, it is impossible for us to meet. I have to find out what grounds my solicitor has for his sudden action and of course your father – or rather Q as I only know him and think of him.

Of course this was merely a delay in the now inevitable meeting between Wilde and Bosie.

Five days after cancelling their plans due to legal reasons, Wilde had managed to pull himself out of the doldrums and celebrated Queen Victoria's Jubilee with a tea party at his villa. There were traditional English tea delights including strawberries and cream and a large cake decorated with pink icing with the words '*Jubilé de la Reine Victoria*' for the local schoolchildren and their teacher. This day of jollity with the local children must have been hard for Oscar, as he missed his own boys greatly.

Wilde wrote to Bosie on 23 June 1897:

> My darling Boy, Thanks for your letter received this morning. My fete was a huge success: fifteen gamins were entertained on strawberries and cream, apricots, chocolates, cakes and sirop de grenadine. I had a huge iced cake with Jubilé de la Reine Victoria ... they sang the Marseilles and other songs

Wilde was true to form as he was extremely generous as each child left with either an accordion, trumpet or clarinet, and a slice of cake and bonbons.

It was about this time that Oscar started to work on *The Ballad of Reading Gaol*, a beautifully worded poem in the style of a ballad about one of the men serving time and awaiting execution for the murder of his wife. Despite the topic of the poem, it is one of the most beautiful and moving pieces of poetry written. This was the only work Oscar produced following his release from prison, and he certainly finished his career with one his best pieces of writing. It would be a labour of love that would take the full summer and into October of 1897 to finish. When finally completed, the ballad was 600 lines long.

While Wilde was working on *The Ballad of Reading Gaol*, he also started to think about other possible plays. Two ideas that he considered were plays like *Salomé*, inspired by stories in the Bible. The first was based around the biblical story of Moses, the Pharaoh and the plagues. It is easy to see the attraction for that Old Testament Story and its potential to be staged. The second play idea was closer in theme to *Salomé*, as it would be based upon the story of Ahab and that other scandalous women of the Old Testament, Jezebel. He even went as far as imagining his friend Sarah Bernhardt as Jezebel. Sadly, neither play was even started.

In August of 1897 Robbie Ross came alone to visit Oscar in Normandy. At some point during the visit, the pair slept together. A lost, lonely Wilde, finding his post-prison life harder to adjust to that he had expected, would have felt comfort in the familiar pleasure that he had enjoyed with Ross and others prior to his arrest. However, Ross had also unwittingly made Bosie even more tempting to Wilde.

Wilde and Bosie once again tried to arrange to meet up in person. After ruling out Paris, as Wilde was still uncomfortable about facing Parisian society, the pair decided to meet in the Normandy city of Rouen.

This time there was no solicitor's warning and Oscar and Bosie were reunited at la Gare de Rouen. Upon seeing Bosie on the station platform, Wilde broke down and cried – the pair had not seen each other in twenty-eight months. They spent a day and a night together in Rouen. Neither side held grudges, it was as if the last twenty-eight months had never happened. Wilde acknowledges the meeting at the end of a letter dated 31 August:

> Everyone is furious with me for going back to you, but they don't understand us. I feel that it is only with you that I can do anything at all. Do remake my ruined life for me, and then our friendship and love will have a different meaning to the world. I wish that when we met at Rouen we had not parted at all. There are such wide abysses now of space and land between us. But we love each other. Goodnight dear.
>
> Ever yours
> Oscar

Although Wilde did not advertise that he was going to meet Bosie in Rouen, it soon became knowledge to all who mattered. Wilde and Bosie were unfortunate enough to run into another of Wilde's friends, Reggie Turner, in Rouen. Reggie, of course, told their other friends. One of the people who were 'furious' at Wilde was Robbie Ross. Wilde admits to meeting Bosie in a letter to Ross of 4 September:

> I am delighted you have come back, as you will now be able to join me in Rouen – Hôtel d'Angleterre. I go in half an hour. I simply cannot stand Berneval .... Yes I saw Bosie,

and of course I love him as I always did, with a sense of tragedy and ruin. He was on his best behaviour and very sweet. Do come to Rouen at once.

> Ever yours
> Oscar

When Bosie and Wilde met up in late August it seems that they had discussed future plans, one of which going to Naples for the rest of the year and renting a villa. Soon after relocating to Hôtel d'Angleterre, Wilde started to make plans for a trip to Naples.

While Oscar had relocated to Rouen, Bosie had met up with his mother and sister to take the spa waters at Aix-les-Bains. He hoped that the water treatments at the spa might help with rheumatic pain. Wilde writes to Bosie to finalise the plans for Naples on 12 September 1899:

> My dearest boy, I hope to go to Naples in three days, but I must try and get some more money. I see it costs £10 to get to Naples. This is awful. Of course, wait until your cure is finished …. But the sooner you come to Naples the happier I shall be.

Oscar's financial issues were temporarily elevated by the arrival of his £15 allowance from Constance, and a cheque for a further £15 from his friend Mr Rothenstein. He also managed to 'borrow' 100 francs from his neighbours in Normandy. The first leg of the journey was to get to Paris, where an old friend, Vincent O'Sullivan, paid for his ticket to Naples. Bosie eventually joined Oscar on the train at Aix-les-Bains and they travelled on to Naples together. Oscar and Bosie arrived in Naples in mid-September. In recent years Naples had become a popular winter destination for the well off due to its warm climate and sunshine. To start with the pair checked into the grand – and somewhat out of their limited budget – Hôtel Royal des Etrangers, located on the waterfront giving views of Capri, Vesuvius and the idyllic bay of Naples. Between them they managed to accrue a bill totalling £68 (roughly £5,316 today).

Oscar had arranged for his mail from Normandy and Paris to be forwarded on to Naples and among the correspondence waiting for him was a letter from Constance. In the letter she invites him to come stay with at her Genoa home, Villa Elvira. She also included pictures of the children for him. Oscar felt it was cruel of Constance to invite in at this point as it was mid-September and Cyril and Vyvyan would have returned to their boarding schools. It was the children, more than his estranged wife, that he wanted to see. This invitation, four months after his release from prison, was too little too late for Oscar. He had already started to make a new life and had fallen into bad habits in the bad company of Bosie.

In fairness to Wilde, he expresses repeatedly in letters to other correspondences and friends that he doesn't blame Constance for her distance. He also acknowledges that his behaviour had not be acceptable in the years leading up to 1895, and that this was the consequence of his actions. That is not to say he was not disappointed and frustrated at not being able to see his beloved sons.

Oscar replied to Constance's letter requesting that they delay the visit for several weeks. Given his circumstances and his request to delay any visit, Constance suspected that he was with Bosie again. She had be told that Bosie was on Capri and so, in her next letter, questioned her husband about whether he had visited that 'appalling individual', as well as accusing him of not caring for the boys as he had not acknowledged the pictures of them included in her previous letter. This accusation would have stung Wilde.

Equally unhappy at Wilde were Robbie Ross and Reggie Turner, who both knew for certain that Wilde and Bosie were together. Both wrote to Wilde expressing their concern. Wilde addresses the issue with Bosie in two correspondences to Ross. The first, on 21 September:

Tuesday 21 September 1897   Hôtel Royal des Etrangers

My dearest Robbie, Your letter has reached me here. My going back to Bosie was psychologically inevitable: and setting aside the interior life of soul with its passion for self-realisation at all costs, the world forced it on me. I cannot live without the atmosphere of Love: I must love and be loved, whatever price I pay for it. I could have lived all my life with you, but you have other claims on you ... all you could offer me was a week of companionship ... The world shuts its gateway against me, and the door of Love lies open.

After everything that Robbie Ross had done for Wilde before, during and after his trial and imprisonment, this was an ungrateful and rather spiteful letter. Yet it seems he did not give up on his friend. Ross seems to have replied to this letter several times before Wilde replies to him on 1 October 1897:

Friday 1 October 1897   Villa Giudice, Posilippo, Naples

Dearest Robbie, I have not answered your letters, because they distressed me and angered me, and I did not wish to write to you of all people in the world in an angry mood, you have been such a good friend to me. Your love, your generosity, your care of me in prison and out of prison are the most lovely things in my life. Without you what would I have done? As you remade my life for me you have the perfect right to say what you choose to me, but I have no right to say anything to you except to tell you how grateful I am to you and what pleasure it is to feel gratitude and love at the same time for the same person. I dare say what I have done is fatal, but it had to be done.

Thankfully, Wilde's second letter was apologetic in nature. At the time of writing this letter, Oscar would have been with Bosie in Naples for over two weeks. It is fair to assume the 'sweet' and 'best behaviour' of

Rouen, had long since faded. If one of Wilde's faults was his readiness to forgive and to be used by Bosie, one of his finest traits was the ability to self-reflect and accept he may have made a big mistake.

It wasn't just Wilde's friends that were unhappy with the lovers' reunion. Bosie's mother was also unimpressed with the arrangement. She had counted upon the pairs' imposed separation as a means for her son's connection to Wilde to diminish.

Eventually Constance did find out that her husband was living with Bosie in Naples and her response was to write to him. The contents of her letter are retold by Wilde in correspondence with Robbie Ross on 3 October:

> She [Constance] wrote me a terrible letter, but a foolish one, saying 'I forbid you' to do and so 'I will not allow you' etc and 'I require a distinct promise that you will not' etc. How can she really imagine that she can influence or control my life? … It makes one laugh. So I suppose she will now try to deprive me of my wretched £3 a week. Women are so petty, and Constance has no imagination …. I don't meddle in her life. I accept the separation from the children: I acquiesce. Why does she want to go on bothering me, and trying to ruin me?

After an expensive and over indulgent week at the hotel in Naples, the pair had rented Villa Giudice, located in Posilippo, Naples. They had paid four months' rent up front. The idea was that the villa would become a writing sanctuary were they both could be creative and be together. During this time Wilde did in fact complete *The Ballad of Reading Gaol*, but any other hopes of creative inspiration, particularly in regards to writing a new play, were never to be realised. Wilde had sold *The Ballad of Reading Gaol* to British publishers Leonard Smithers, but struggled to find an American publisher willing to publish the long poem. It was decided to wait until the new year of 1898 to publish the poem, because given the author and the poem's theme, it was not considered suitable as a Christmas gift.

The pair had planned a three-day trip to the small island of Capri, located in the Bay of Naples. This was because Oscar wanted to lay flowers on the grave of Tiberius. However, the trip was nothing short of a disaster. On the first evening, when the pair were seated in Hôtel Quisisana's restaurant, they hadn't even start their meal before the hotel manager asked them to leave. A second hotel was tried but they were turned away again. Thankfully, as they were trying to work out what to do, an acquaintance of Bosie's spotted them looking lost in a piazza. The friend was Dr Axel Munthe, who upon hearing their troubles invited them to stay at his home for the night. The following day Wilde went straight back to Naples, while Bosie, ignoring Wilde's discomfort, chose to stay and catch up with other friends.

As well as being a warmer climate than northern France, Wilde and Bosie most likely chose Naples for the fact that the city had something of a reputation for offering a multitude of sexual delights for a variety of tastes and sexualities. Bosie had visited the city and indulged in the delights that were on offer and just as he had done in London, he now wanted to introduce Oscar to these Neapolitan delectations. However, this return to hedonistic fun was short lived as the local press had noticed Wilde's rendezvous with Neapolitan youths. In a similar vein, Wilde enjoyed visiting the cities Museo Nazionale, which houses many of the risqué artefacts and finds from both Pompeii and Herculaneum.

It would be Bosie's mother who would succeed – where her now ex-husband, the Marquess of Queensberry had failed – in finally bringing the short-lived reunion to an end. Life at Villa Giudice was not exactly smooth sailing, any honeymoon period had long diminished after two months of Wilde and Bosie living under the same roof. Bosie was angry because Wilde was not writing plays to be sold for good money. He had expected Wilde to write as he had done prior to going to prison and at the height of his fame. The constant pressure of money worries caused arguments. Then there was that added stress due to the interest in the villa and its inhabitants by the local press. Both came to the conclusion that their relationship had changed, neither could remake what they'd had before 1895. Both, however, were reluctant to end the reunion or living arrangements.

Then Bosie then received two letters, one from his brother and the other his mother. Both letters asked Bosie to leave Wilde, and in the case of his mother's letter, she threatened to cut off his allowance if he did not comply with her request. This gave both Oscar and Bosie a justifiable cause to separate and save face in doing so. Having both argued and defended their reunion, neither wanted it to look like it had failed – this way they could blame their parting of the ways on Lady Queensberry's demands.

Bosie agreed to leave Naples if his mother could arrange money for Wilde in lieu of the debt, his father's court case had caused Wilde. Lady Queensberry promised Oscar £200, on the condition that they never lived together again. She sent £68 as her first instalment which was used to pay the debt they had run up at Hôtel Royal des Etrangers. By the end of the first week of December 1897, Bosie had left Wilde, their villa, and Naples behind.

Despite having been unhappy with Bosie, Wilde fell into a depressive episode and wallowed in self-pity. He even went to sit in a Neapolitan park favoured by the locals as a suicide spot. While sitting there, he came to the conclusion that suicide would not help him find peace. He disliked the thought that he would be stuck in that park for eternity, it was a prospect he did not like and it was enough to put him off doing anything to harm himself.

It is about this time that Wilde found solace through drinking. He had always been able to hold his drink well, partly due to his stature. But now he turned to alcohol to numb his feelings. It was a habit that would stay with him for the last two years of his life.

That festive season, Wilde escaped to Taormina on the Italian island of Sicily, where he stayed at the Hôtel Victoria. While he was there, he met Albert Stopford, a young man who had left London in 1894 in order to escape being arrested for the same offence as Wilde, gross indecency.

The new year did not start well for Wilde; upon returning to the rented Villa Giudice he discovered that the servants had stolen his clothes and some of his belongings. This was made even worse when he came down with a bout of influenza. Once recovered he decided to relocate back into the centre of Naples and away from the Villa and its frustrating and sad memories. He did not stay in central Naples long, as by early February he had relocated to the place that would be his last home, Paris.

This chapter of Wilde's life was particularly tragic, whatever he had imagined freedom to have been, it surely was not the reality of the last seven months of 1897. By February 1898 it seems that he had almost given up and could not find a way to resurrect his writing; without his work, Oscar was lost. His behaviour and association with Bosie had finally ended any hoped of reconciliation with his estranged wife and his boys and he was far from his friends. Wilde looked to Paris as his last hope for happiness.

THE FINAL CURTAIN CALL

'My wallpaper and I are fighting a duel to the death.
One or the other of us has got to go.'

Oscar Wilde

Wilde left Naples and arrived in Paris halfway through February 1898. On 13 February, Smithers had published *The Ballad of Reading Gaol*. Due to the title, the use of Wilde's prison number C.3.3 didn't really fool any one – it was something of an open secret. The poem was met with positivity and was nothing short of a success. Within the first week it had sold all of the 1,000, copies.

Robie Ross sent Oscar over all the positive press cuttings when he next wrote to his friend. It must have pleased Oscar that the governor of Reading Gaol, Major Neilson, thought it was a wonderful piece of poetry. Even his estranged wife thought the poem was beautiful.

As well as several new print runs of the poem, ninety-nine special author's editions were produced and had been skilfully illustrated and signed. These special books were sold at half a guinea. By the end of May 1898, 5,000 copies had been printed to meet demand.

Wilde's arrival in Paris coincided with one of the biggest political and legal dramas in French History – The Dreyfus affair. Captain Alfred Dreyfus a Jewish French army officer had been tried and found guilty of spying and giving the Germans military intelligence in 1894. His sentence was to live out the rest of his life on the penal colony of Devil's Island. By 1898, there had been investigations that cast doubt on Dreyfus's guilt. Unwittingly, Oscar found himself playing a role in helping secure a retrial for Dreyfus.

During his time in Paris, Wilde was in the company of the man who really had spied and passed on information to the Germans, Major Esterhazy. At one of their meetings Esterhazy allegedly said, 'We are the two greatest martyrs in all humanity, but I have suffered more'. Acquaintances advised Wilde not to socialise with the controversial Major, and Oscar is said to have responded: 'If Esterhazy were innocent, I should have nothing to do with him'.

Wilde had found out secret details of the case from his friend Carlos Blacker, who knew someone with inside knowledge. Wilde passed this information on to a young Dreyfusard – the popular term for a supporter of Dreyfus – called Chris Healy, who in turn passed this information on to Émile Zola. The exact details of the information Wilde received is not known, but it was enough for Zola and the Dreyfusards to have the case at again, and for Dreyfus to be retried and found not guilty.

Zola had learnt where the information had come from and sought to meet with Wilde. However, Wilde refused to meet with the French novelist. He was still angry that Zola would not sign a petition in Paris against his trial and conviction in 1895.

Money was still tight, but Constance had started to pay her husband his allowance again as he was no longer living with Bosie. This source of income would not last, as in April of that year, Constance died from complications following a surgery in Switzerland. The initial shock of the news was greatly distressing to Oscar.

Not long after Constance's death, Oscar had his own health scare. In May 1898, he required surgery for 'quinsy' – an abscess on the tonsils that requires their removal. Throughout the procedure Wilde was under the influence of cocaine rather than chloroform.

Although they had parted ways under a slight cloud, Bosie had come to Paris and he and Wilde met up, though only as friends. After a year of freedom, Oscar had started to slip into a depression that was affecting his ability to write anything. He is even said to have referred to the *Ballad Of Reading Gaol* as his '*chant de cygne*', his swansong.

Financially, he was still living a somewhat hand-to-mouth existence. When he had money he spent it on treats and indulgences to cheer himself up, one of his favourites being cologne at one of Paris's finest perfumeries of the day, Jules & Roger. This often left him short of cash at the end of the month and needing to beg money from friends and acquaintances.

One of the few friends that he made in Paris was the bohemian artist of the Moulin Rouge nightclub, Henri de Toulouse-Lautrec. They must have made a funny sight out together Wilde, with being of above average hight alongside the artist's petite statue.

Frank Harris, like many of his friends, had started to grow worried about Oscar and felt that he needed to try to write again. Harris made Oscar a very generous offer, to go to the south of France as his guest while he looked into buying a small hotel in the area. Oscar agreed. Harris put Oscar up in hotel in a small fishing village called Napoule. Unfortunately, this did nothing to encourage Wilde in his writing. His days were spent reading, shopping and writing letters, and the evenings were spent picking up rent boys. When Harris asked about his writing, Wilde felt harassed and henpecked.

Wilde was invited to Switzerland by Harold Mellor for the month and he gratefully accepted to get away from Harris and his nagging about work. He did go to Genoa en route to Switzerland to visit the Constance's grave. In a letter dated 1 March 1900, Wilde tells Robbie Ross of his visit:

> I went to Genoa to see Constance's grave. It is very pretty – a marble cross with dark ivy-leaves inlaid in a good pattern. The cemetery is a garden at the foot of lovely hills that climb into the mountains that girdle Genoa. It was very tragic seeing her name carved on a tomb – her surname, my name, not mentioned of course … I brought some flowers. I was deeply affected – with a sense, also, of the uselessness of all regrets.

Wilde would get more sad news while he was in Switzerland with Mellor. His brother Willie had died in London on 13 March 1899, aged just 46.

Poor Oscar. All the time he had become more and more depressed and was finding solace in drinking to help him escape his misery.

In April, Oscar took his leave of Harold Mellor and decided to head to the Italian Riviera but this novelty soon wore off. He once again found himself penniless and unable to pay to get back to Paris.

Wilde had, at some point since his release, spoken to a man called Sledger and mentioned something about a new play. Nothing was signed, but Sledger got impatient when no script materialised. He then passed the project on to an acquaintance called Roberts. He met with Wilde's publisher and the pair of them decided to go out to the Italian Rivera and make a deal in person with Oscar.

The three met at Cafe Concordia and a deal was made that Roberts would pay Wilde £100 for each completed and submitted act of the play. After having met Wilde and once he had returned to the UK, Roberts was unsure about his decision and so offered Smithers the opportunity to buy the contract with Wilde. Smithers agreed and issued Wilde with even better terms and conditions than Roberts had.

Smithers offered to pay some of Wilde's debts, pay for a train ticket back to Paris and give him a weekly allowance so that he could write the play. This was very generous, especially given he had failed to write anything after *The Ballad of Reading Gaol*. Wilde gratefully accepted this new deal.

Then disaster struck; Wilde became ill. Robbie Ross came to his aid again and got a woeful Wilde back to Paris. Ross told Wilde that his illness was due to heavy drinking. This grave warning from Ross made Wilde temporarily abstain from alcohol, but this did not last long.

Wilde stayed just outside of Paris at a place called Chennevières-sur-Marne for the summer of 1899. At the end of the summer, Wilde took lodgings at Hôtel d'Alsace. He once again fell into a regular routine of staying out late with rent boys and staying in bed until lunchtime, cadging lunch from friends and drinking far too much.

By the start of 1900 and the dawn of the twentieth century, Wilde was, not surprisingly, unwell again. His depressive state was just getting worse not helped by the large quantities of alcohol used to self-medicate.

He had also developed a strange looking skin eruption. The rash was both itchy and mottled looking. This was added to by a nasty prolonged bout of streptococcal (strep) throat that caused sepsis and ten days in a hospital.

In early spring of 1900 Wilde took a last trip to Italy with Harold Mellor and they visited Rome, Naples and Sicily. The Rome part of the trip happened to fall close to Easter. He also met up with Robbie Ross, who was there with his mother. Wilde was once again captivated by the Catholic Church and would receive seven blessings from Pope Leo XIII. According to Oscar, these blessings 'cured his itchy rash'. When Ross and Mellor had both departed, Wilde stayed on in the Italian capital. He had acquired an early camera and he was enjoying taking pictures of the sights in the eternal city.

Wilde returned to Paris and Hôtel d'Alsace in May and would take in the delights of the Exposition Universelle, marvelling at the inventions and machines. There is grainy film showing Wilde seeing what the great exposition had to offer. Wilde enjoyed visiting the various country's exhibits – experiencing all there was to see, do and taste. From innovative, new inventions, to cultural displays and older art works everything captured his attention and brought him joy. One of his favourites was the Rodin pavilion where the artist himself was often present.

Thankfully, Oscar was not without friends. George Alexander, a manager and actor known to Wilde through his theatre work and the circles he had moved at the peak of his success, came to Paris with his wife. While there he offered to help his friend financially and an arrangement was put in place that Oscar received £20 per month via Robbie Ross. This was an extremely generous and kind offer.

Like many Parisians, Wilde took daytrips away from the summer heat in the city, including to former French former royal residence of Fontainebleau, while also meeting his old friends, including actress Ellen Terry, during those last few months of his life. It was while he was among his oldest friends, that he was able to relax and his trademark wit once again began to flow as it had at the height of his notoriety and fame – even if he now required a little help from a drink or two.

Wilde was in contact with Bosie, who was also in Paris during this time – spending his inheritance from his father, who had died in January 1900. He was enjoying the races and partying like a true Parisian left-bank bohemian. It was during a dinner with Bosie that Wilde made the gloomy prediction that he felt he did not have long to live – a prediction that would sadly turn out to be correct.

During mid-September 1900, Wilde's problematic ear had started to cause him pain again. He consulted a new trendy doctor among the English speaking expatriate community in Paris; his name was Dr Maurice a'Court Tucker. Unfortunately, Dr Tucker underestimated the severity of Oscar's affliction and was only Oscar's physician from 24 September until mid-October, when he recommended that Wilde consult a specialist otologist. Given that his father had been an acclaimed specialist in this area, it is surprising Oscar had not thought to consult an expert before this point.

The infection had spread to more of Wilde's ear and if left untreated could progress to the brain. He was advised that he required an urgent operation to limit the spread. The procedure took place on 10 October in Wilde's hotel room at Hôtel d'Alsace, St Germain de Prés, Paris. Thankfully anaesthetic was used, but it would not have been as effective as modern forms of putting a patient under anaesthetic.

The surgeon removed the infected tissue from Wilde's inner ear so that the infected and diseased tissue could no long spread and cause pain. Initially it was thought that the operation had been a success. In the days after his procedure, Wilde was cared for again by Dr Tucker with the assistance of a local male hospital nurse, who changed his dressings and administered pain relief as required.

The treatment and operation and post-operative care and medications were a further financial burden to the already impoverished Wilde. The surgeon's bill had been £60, however Dr Tucker managed to halve that – whether he paid half himself or spoke to the surgeon it is not clear. His post-operative care and pharmacy bill also grew, and was soon at £20.

As Wilde grew stronger boredom set in and he wrote to Robbie Ross, imploring his friend to come to Paris to be with him. Ross arrived in the city on 17 October, a week after Wilde's operation and a day after his last birthday, he had just turned 46 years old. Robbie Ross was somewhat relieved to find Oscar in improved spirits since their last meeting. Soon he was not Oscar's only visitor. Reggie Turner had also come to Paris; it must have felt like the days before he had gone to jail for Oscar.

Unfortunately, old habits did not fade and inevitably Wilde consumed large qualities of champagne and good French cuisine. Given that his health was still delicate this would not have been a prudent course of action for his recovery. Although the poet put on a show of good mental spirits, he still looked ill and this worsened when his irritating skin condition returned, causing him to constantly scratch the rash.

He was panic-stricken about his ever-growing debts. Near the end of his life it is thought that he owed close to £400 to various people and establishments, including the hotel he was staying in. That is roughly the equivalent of £31,268 today. Ross decided to write to Bosie to tell him of Oscar's condition and dire financial situation in the hope that he would be able to help his old lover and friend out and elevate some of his anxieties. This did not happen.

This growing anxiety and melancholia would not have been helped by Wilde's reluctance to get out of his bed after his operation. Then, out of the blue, on 29 October, after nineteen days' convalescence, Oscar not only got out of his bed but decided to leave the hotel. He and Ross visited a local bistro where he over-indulged in that most bohemian drink of Paris, absinthe. Noted not only for its very high alcohol content, one of the drink's main ingredients was the compound of thujone, found in wormwood. The effect of thujone was to give the drinker hallucinations, while its high alcoholic percentage – varying from 45–75% proof, could be attributed to addiction to the beverage by some of its drinkers. Although Wilde was far from the only fan of absinthe, his indulgence would not have helped his post-operative recovery. As a consequence, he spent 30 October in bed recovering, but he did not linger longer than necessary and the following day was out again driving with Ross towards Bois de Boulogne, a large public park to the west of Paris. Once again, when they stopped for refreshment, Wilde indulged in absinthe.

Having rushed to be with Oscar, Robbie Ross felt that Wilde had recovered sufficiently enough for him not cancel his long-standing plans to spend the winter in Nice. He planned to leave Oscar and Paris in mid-November. Just before he was due to leave Oscar suffered a sudden and excruciating relapse, the infection in his ear had returned with a vengeance. Dr Tucker and his nurse administered morphine, while Wilde tried to ease the pain with champagne. Wilde tried to persuade Ross to stay in Paris but to no avail, he was convinced Oscar was being over-dramatic.

After Ross departed for the south of France, Reggie Turner took over caring for their friend. Regular pain relief from morphine caused him to be lethargic and affected his spirits. In this final illness he was moved to room 13 of the Hôtel d'Alsace. By the evening of 24 November Oscar's condition had deteriorated to the point that it was clear he was unlikely to recover and that his life was coming to an end. The infection, despite the operation, had now reached Wilde's brain, there was no doubt that the diagnosis was meningoencephalitis. Turner wrote urgently to Ross, informing him of Oscar's prognosis.

Ross returned to Paris on 29 November. Upon, arrival at Hôtel d'Alsace he found his friend in a terrible state. His once larger-than-life figure was now skin and bones and part of his head had been shaved so that the doctors could apply leeches. (Although this practice was less widely used in the late nineteenth century, it was still used occasionally as late as 1900). Upon seeing Oscar in such a state, he asked his friend if he should find a Catholic priest. Oscar, unable to speak, raised a hand in assent.

That afternoon, around four o'clock, Robbie Ross returned to Hôtel d'Alsace with Father Cuthbert Dunne. During the time Ross went to fetch a priest, Wilde had started to slip in and out of consciousness. Fr Dunne explained what he would do and although he could no longer speak Wilde was able to communicate using hand signs that consented to conversion and baptism into the Catholic faith, something that his mother would have approved of.

After Fr Dunne had finished with Wilde, Robbie Ross started informing everyone he thought needed to know of Wilde's impending death. Telegraphs were sent to his solicitor, Holman, so that the news could be broken to Oscar's sons, Cyril and Vyvyan. Ross also telegrammed Bosie, who was currently on holiday in Scotland.

Around 5.30 am, the final phase of dying came over Oscar. Once again Fr Dunne was summoned for the last rights and sacrament of extreme unction. Oscar Wilde died in room 13 of Hôtel d'Alsace, holding the hand of his most loyal friend, Robbie Ross. He breathed his last at 1.50 pm, on 30 November 1900.

Oscar Fingal O'Flahertie Wills Wilde's funeral was held on 3 December 1900. It was a small, private affair officiated by Fr Cuthbert Dunne at the Parisian church of Saint-Germain-des-Prés in the *6e arrondissement*. There were fifty-six people in the congregation. Among those gathered were the staff who worked at Hôtel d'Alsace, his final home. His coffin was adorned with a wreath of laurel leaves. Although he had missed Oscar's deathbed, the chief mourner at his funeral was Bosie, who had rushed to Paris for the funeral from his Scottish shooting holiday.

Both Wilde's death and funeral did not attract major public or media attention. The notices and obituary in *The Times* were superficial and cursory. Given his notoriety at the height of his fame and success, this is a sad end for one of our literary greats.

Immediately after the funeral service Wilde's coffin was brought to Cimetière de Bagneux in the south-west outskirts of Paris. His remains laid there until 1909 when he was relocated to the prestigious Cimetière de Pere Lachaise. Robbie Ross commissioned the artist Jacob Epstein to create a memorial for his grave at the cost of a staggering £2,000 – approximately £156,000 today. Even in death, Wilde was able to cause scandal while being extravagant and excessive – he was in death as he had been in life. The monument erected by Epstein was considered deviant and inappropriate by the French, as the angel had male genitals displayed. It caused so much outrage that it was covered up by the

French. In 1961, in an act of vandalism, the genitalia on the winged angel, were detached from the monument. Rumour was that the manager of Cimetière Pere Lachaise used the removed part of the monument as a paperweight in his office. Regardless of whether this is true or not, the whereabouts of the controversial stone genitals taken from the angel are unknown today.

Officially Wilde's grave and monument in Pere Lachaise is considered to be an Irish monument overseas, and is therefore cared for by the Irish Government. In 2014 the lower part of the grave monument was protected by a glass barrier to prevent the thousands of fans that visit his resting place from kissing the monument. The lipstick prints left by fans contained ingredients that were harmful to the tombs' stone.

WILDE'S LEGACIES:
HIS SONS AND HIS WORK

'Children begin by loving their parents; as
they grow older they judge them;
sometimes they forgive them.'

The Picture of Dorian Gray

During his marriage to Constance Lloyd, Oscar fathered two sons, Cyril (5 June 1885 – 9 May 1915) and Vyvyan (3 November 1886 – 10 October 1967). Both sons were born in the family home in Tite Street, Chelsea. The building then was at number 16. The street has since be renumbered and is now number property 34. The top floor of the Wildes' house was mostly left for the two boys' use and consisted of a day nursery, a night nursery and bathroom.

In a similar vein to their father's unconventional upbringing, the Wilde boys would often meet the who's who of the London acting, literary and artistic world in their own home. This included regular visits from James McNeill Whistler, John Ruskin, John Singer Sargent, actresses Sarah Bernhardt, Ellen Terry and Lillie Langtry to name but a few.

The sad reality was that Cyril and Vyvyan only knew their father until the spring of 1895, and it was not until Vyvyan's university years that he really read his father's writing and works and got to know his father's old friends and acquaintances. During those early years, although often absent for work and later pleasure, when Oscar was at home he was a most loving, and in many ways a modern, father compared to the traditional stereotype of Victorian fathers.

There is a wonderful childhood memory recorded by Vyvyan on page 53 of his autobiography *Son of Oscar Wilde*:

> One day he arrived with a toy milk cart drawn by a horse with real hair … and the churns with which the cart was full … When my father discovered this he immediately went down stairs and came back with a jug of milk with which he proceeded to fill the churns.

Another part of parenting that Oscar greatly enjoyed was telling his sons fairy stories, many of which were of his own invention. In his autobiography, Vyvyan says that the last gift his father gave him was a copy of Rudyard Kipling's *Jungle Book*, and that his father had previously gifted him Robert Louis Stephenson's *Treasure Island* and Jules Verne's *Five Weeks in a Balloon*. It should also come as no surprise that Oscar enjoyed playing with the children when they visited the seaside. Vyvyan says that his father's sandcastles were extravagant, complete with moats, towers, battlements and tunnels, and he would often produce lead soldiers to patrol the battlements of these castles. (V Holland, *Son of Oscar Wilde* p.55) By all accounts these early days of childhood were more affluent than many, though this would not continue after 1895.

The consequences of this legal scandal following Wilde's prosecution for gross indecency did not just affect their father but the whole family, including his wife and children.

Initially Constance and the children were going to go to Oscar's homeland, Ireland. In the end only Cyril went to stay with some cousins in Ireland while Vyvyan stayed with his mother in London. However, it soon became apparent that Ireland was just as hostile towards the Wildes as London had become. It was decided that the children would head to Europe with a governess while Constance initially stayed in London to help Oscar and sort out her future. Constance had contacts on the European mainland, most notably her brother Otho Lloyd, who was based in Switzerland.

While in Ireland, Cyril discovered out the truth of his father's trial and 'crimes', and Vyvyan says that his brother was no longer a happy child afterwards. Once Cyril was brought back from his Irish cousins, the two boys and a French governess were sent to France. The journey in April 1895 would take several days and several changes of mode of transport. First there was a train to Dover then a ferry to Calais. The crossing over the channel was slightly rough, rendering the governess and Cyril unwell while Vyvyan explored the ship. Vyvyan found himself in the engine room watching how it worked. From Calais the party of three travelled to Paris via train. It was the second of two long boring train journeys. In the haste to get the boys off to Europe only essentials had been packed and the boys had nothing to do or distract them on these train journeys. Eventually they arrived, late in the evening, at their hotel on the left bank of the Siene. Once at the hotel the boys were given a supper of bread, butter and coffee before the governess put them to bed.

The journey continued the next day. The governess roused the boys, and following breakfast left them in the hotel reception with their luggage while she went out, only returning in the afternoon. Later that afternoon the party took a train to Geneva from Gare l'Est which would be the longest of all the train journeys at sixteen hours. From Geneva the boys and their governess took a small local train to bring them to their final destination, for the time being, the small town of Montreux.

In Montreux the party of three were booked into the Hôtel du Righi-Vaudois while they waited for Constance to join them. In those weeks as they waited for their mother, Cyril and Vyvyan lived a carefree life enjoying the local Montreux countryside. Eventually Constance joined her boys in late May and the lazy governess was swiftly dismissed. However, within days of arriving at Hôtel du Righi-Vaudois, news of Oscar's conviction had reached the Switzerland and the hotel manager asked the family to leave the hotel. The family relocated to the Ligurian coast of Italy were Constance had some friends, most notably Margaret Brooke, who held the title of Ranee of Sarawak. Once here, Constance had time to decide what to do next to look after her boys.

After their brief stay on the Ligurian coast, Constance and the boys travelled to Switzerland to join her brother Otho and his family in Swiss village of Bevaix. Once there the boys had a more routine life after months of carefree living, as their uncle Otho implemented an informal education with his nephews.

There was another big change in store for Cyril and Vyvyan. After the family had been asked to leave the Hôtel du Righi-Vaudois Constance had started the legal process of changing her and the boys surnames to Holland, an old family name. Holland was considered safer than Lloyd, Constance's maiden name. Vyvyan also had to change the less common way he spelt his first name. For the rest of his education, he would spell his name Vivian, but would change the spelling back to Vyvyan as an adult. All three of them kept the surname Holland until their respective deaths in 1898, 1915 and 1967.

The Hollands spend the rest of the summer and into September with Otho before returning to the Ligurian coast, accompanied by Otho and his family so that Constance could be near her friend, the Ranee of Sarawak. The two families shared a big villa in a fishing village. During this time Otho continued to try to educate his freedom-loving nephews in the mornings, leaving them the afternoons to explore the locality and countryside. They were still in the north of Italy in February 1896 when Constance needed to return to London in order to tell Oscar that his mother had died. This would also be the last time husband and wife would see each other.

Constance was gone for three weeks and more changes were in store for the boys upon her return. It had been decided that, after months of freedom, Cyril and Vyvyan needed to resume formal education in school. It was, of course, out of the question to send the boys back to the UK, so the Hollands travelled to Germany to Freiburg im Breisgau.

Freiburg im Breisgau was a university town in the Rhenish province of the recently unified Germany. In his autobiography, Vyvyan was unable to remember the name of the first two schools they were enrolled in. Neither school worked out. Both boys struggled to settle into the regimented routine of a boarding school. At the first German school one of the masters attempted to punish Vyvyan, and Cyril decided to intervene and attacked the master. The second German school lasted roughly the same amount of time, this time this issue was with their German peers who, even at this time, were very anti-British. The Holland brothers took offence at the taunts from their classmates and challenged their peers to a fight. Again the result of this incident resulted in the boys being expelled from the school.

It was then decided that the boys should attend an English school rather than a German school and the family relocated to Heidelberg where there was a large British expat community, and a couple of English schools for the expats to choose from. Both boys started at Neuenheim College in April 1896.

Although Neuenheim College was an improvement upon the German schools, it was still a difficult adjustment for the boys, especially Vyvyan. During that first summer term the boys were able to once again take part in team sports, most importantly cricket.

Their cricketing whites had been brought with them from England but had not been needed until now. When the names had been changed on the boys' clothes and possessions, the cricket whites were overlooked and so still had Wilde as their surname. Cyril came to the rescue and removed the boys' nametags in the school bathroom using his pocket knife. (*Son of Oscar Wilde* p.94) But it was a reminder to both brothers that they had to be careful not to disclose their former identities, accidentally or otherwise.

When the school term ended, Constance took the boys to a hotel located in the Black Forest for their break. Because of their new identities they were left in peace at Hôtel Schloss. At the end of that particular school break, Constance took both boys down to Heidelberg dressed in their Eton suits to have their picture taken professionally. Copies of these photographs were sent to Oscar, who kept them on his person until he died. According to Robert Ross, Oscar would often look at them and wonder out loud how they both were.

When the new academic year of 1896/97 started both brothers returned to Neuenheim College; like many siblings, however, the brothers had started to drift apart from each other and Vyvyan was still not settling into life at school. He got through that first term but confided to his mother during the festive break that he was unhappy. For the following term, arrangements were made to send Vyvyan to a new school at the beginning of 1897.

In January 1897 Constance and Vyvyan travelled to the principality of Monaco, located on the French Riviera, very close to the Italian boarder. Vyvyan was then enrolled in to the Jesuit collegio della Visitazione. Monaco was chosen as a location to find Vyvyan a school was partly because Princess Alice of Monaco had been a loyal friend to both Oscar and Constance, even after the scandal of the trial and Oscar's subsequent conviction. She was able to help put Constance's mind at ease, knowing that there was a good friend close by to look out for Vyvyan should he need it. It was also very close to the north of Italy were Constance spent most of her time while the boys were away at school.

There is an interesting history as to why there was an Italian Jesuit school located outside of Italy but close to the border. In 1870 the Jesuit holy order had been banned in Italy by the Vatican, so the good brothers made a new home in Monaco. Most of the pupils of the school were from good Italian families who want to have their sons educated by the Jesuits and so sent them to the Jesuit collegio della Visitazione.

Vyvyan's schooldays under the guidance of the Jesuit brothers in Monaco were far kinder than his days at Neuenheim College. The rhythm of the Jesuits religious day and routine that the boys followed was less likely to foster bullying or the need for corporal punishment. The only real teething problem Vyvyan had was that he didn't speak much Italian. Through his education and travels he had acquired good French and strong German, but had only pleasantries in Italian from his few months on the north Italian coast. However, like many young minds he picked up what he needed quickly and most of the brothers and masters spoke French when required.

One of the conditions set down by the Lloyd family that to allowed Vyvyan to attend a Jesuit Catholic School was that while he was a student there, he was forbidden to convert to the Catholic Church. Constance's family, like Oscar's, were from a Protestant background. This would cause young Vyvyan distress while he was there as he, like his father Oscar, had strong leanings towards the Catholic doctrine. This would be especially hard for Vyvyan on the 21 June, the feast day of St Aloysius of Gonzaga, the traditional day that Italian children make their First Holy Communion. Vyvyan had to watch as his peers undertook this rite of passage. It was during that spring academic term of 1897 that his father was finally released from Reading Gaol.

Vyvyan and Constance took the train to Germany at the start of the school holidays to meet up with Cyril, and the family once again returned to the Black Forest for the break. It would be their last summer with their mother. September came around once again and the boys went their separate ways to their schools. The boys of the Jesuit collegio della Visitazione were required to spend high feast at school and this included Christmas and Easter breaks, when they were expected to take part in all the special masses for the feasts. Having missed the Christmas holidays with her son over 1897/8, Constance visited Vyvyan in February 1898 and was able to take him out of school for a week, staying in a local hotel. Little did they both know that this would be the last time that they saw one and other.

Constance had been in delicate health for a long time and it had worsened just before the scandal of Oscar's trial happened, when she fell down the stairs at Tite Street. She never really fully recovered from that fall. The boys were not really aware of just how unwell their mother was as they were away at school for a large part of the final three years of their mother's life. In February 1898 Constance went in for a relatively routine operation to help alleviate some of the problems, and subsequently died of complications after surgery. Modern historians have debated the nature of Constance's illness and it is most commonly agreed that she was probably suffering from a severe form of Multiple Sclerosis that was probably not helped by the stress she faced in the last five years of her life. She died on 7 April 1898.

The difficult job of telling the 12-year-old Vyvyan the news of his mother's death fell to Fr Stradelli. Upon hearing this he was naturally upset and enquired about his father. Reluctantly, the Jesuit father confirmed to Vyvyan that Oscar had been in prison but was now free. This was the first time in his life that Vyvyan had confirmation of where his father had been since 1895 and why he had not seen him.

With the death of his mother and his father estranged, this would be the final term that Vyvyan spent at the Jesuit collegio della Visitazione. But the brothers would send him home with a prospectus for Stonyhurst College in Lancashire, a Jesuit school, in the hope that he would continue his Catholic education. At the end of that school year of 1897/98, after three years in exile in Europe both boys found themselves back in London and in the care of their mother's family.

Vyvyan was the first of the brothers to arrive back in London, having been escorted to Constance's aunt, Mrs Napier, and her cousin Elizabeth, whom the boys referred to as Lizzie. Mrs Napier lived in Kensington, London, and were legal gardens of Cyril and Vyvyan, though they were also made wards in Chancery. This was more of a formality rather than having any real effect on their upbringing. Since Oscar's disgrace the Lloyd family had been trying to distance Constance and their sons from Oscar and had succeeded, given that the boys last saw their father in 1895 and Constance only saw Oscar twice while he was imprisoned. This attitude towards Wilde continued even after he had been released from prison and their children had lost their mother. Cyril joined Vyvyan at the Napiers a few days later.

Vyvyan gave the Stonyhurst prospective to his relatives once he got home and to his relief they agreed that he could continue his Catholic education. Cyril, it was decided, would attend Radley College, with the understanding that he was likely to take a career in the military. Cyril had always hoped that the Navy would take him, but he would eventually go on to join the Army.

Their mother's family were keen to keep the brothers separated, feeling that it would help keep protect their identity. There was already a greater drift between the boys since they had gone to separate schools in Europe. The family used the fact that Cyril was Protestant and that

Vyvyan was outwardly Catholic as a reason to keep the boys separated further. This did not stop them from writing to each other fairly frequently.

Cyril continued his education at Radley until 1902. Radley had a reputation for athleticism in its students and although Cyril excelled on the sports field he never really enjoyed it, seeing it rather as a means to keep fit in a masculine way. Knowing about his father, and the details of what he was imprisoned for, made Cyril pursue far more masculine career and leisure time compared with Vyvyan. According to Vyvyan's autobiography, when learning about his brother after his death in 1915, his former school peers had had no idea he was the son of Oscar Wilde, and recalled him as a less sociable student who kept himself to himself.

From Radley, Cyril went on to the Royal Military Academy base at Woolwich. From there he pursued a career in the army being posted to India, where he was still stationed just before the onset of the First World War in 1914. He reached the rank of Captain, and would go on to fight on the Western Front, where he was killed by a German sniper on 9 May 1915, during the Battle of Festubert. He was only 29 years old. He was buried in a Commonwealth Grave cemetery in St Vaast, Richebourg-l'Avoué.

In 1898, Vyvyan was not quite old enough to enter Stonyhurst College but was accepted into the college's preparatory school located on the college grounds. This was called Hodder Place. Due to his education with the Jesuit brothers in Monaco, Vyvyan found that with some of his subjects he had a slight advantage, one such subject was Latin, although he had tweak his pronunciation to be slightly more anglicised at Hodder and Stonyhurst. He also found himself at an academic advantage in Mathematics.

Unlike the conditions attached to his attending the Jesuit school in Monaco which forbade Vyvyan to convert to the Catholic faith, this time he was actively encouraged to do so by his guardians. In order to receive his First Holy Communion, Vyvyan had to re-learn all the prayers, mass and catechisms in English rather than Latin, as he had said them in Monaco. He was also baptised. Both Vyvyan and his guardians were not even 100 per cent sure if he had been baptised into the Church of England as an infant; his brother Cyril had been because, unlike Vyvyan, he had a baptism cup. He would eventually make his First Holy Communion on the feast of Corpus Christi, which in the year 1899 fell on 1 June. Oscar who had always flirted with the idea of joining the Catholic Church only did so on his deathbed in 1900, would have fully approved of his youngest son's conviction and conversion to Rome.

Vyvyan flourished academically at Hodder Place but was seen as an outsider by his peers due to his international education and his excellent academic achievements. Given the disruption and tragedy in his life, it is a credit to Vyvyan than he thrived academically and later in life. At the end of the first term at Stonyhurst, Vyvyan gained top marks in all the end of term examinations. This success continued and at the end of that academic year he was in the top percentage of the school and went back to his guardians, the Napiers, with prizes in Mathematics and Classics.

During the summer break of 1899, Vyvyan stayed with one of his mother's friends, Cornelia Cochrane, who lived with her husband in Bagshot. By all accounts his Aunt Neila would become a kindly, much needed mother figure for Vyvyan during that summer.

The first term on the academic year 1900–1 would once again bring tragedy into Vyvyan's young life. For the second time in as many years he was called to see a Jesuit brother and was told one of his parents had died. Thankfully, the Jesuit brother who had this unpleasant task was Fr Joseph Browne – a kindly, well-liked priest. Upon hearing the news, Vyvyan surprised the priest when he said he thought his father was already dead. Gently, the brother said that his father had in fact died in Paris two days earlier, and that he had converted to Rome upon his deathbed, 'So he is happy at last'. In this difficult conversation, the priest told Vyvyan that 'he wrote beautiful stories' (*Son of Oscar Wilde* p.152) that is an extremely kind and compassionate thing for the Catholic brother to have said to Vyvyan, particularly given the nature of the controversy surrounding his father.

Just after Oscar's death, Robert Ross wrote to his friend's sons. It was only later, after Cyril's death, that Ross showed Vyvyan a copy of Cyril's reply to his letter. At the time of writing Cyril was only 15 years old:

> Dear Mr Ross
> It was very kind of you to give flowers for us. I am glad you say that he loved us ... It is of course a long time since I saw my father but all I do remember was when we lived happily together in London.
>
> V Holland, Son of Oscar Wilde, p.153

During 1901 Vyvyan missed the full year of school due to developing a chill in his left ear that turned in to a mastoid requiring an operation. It would take the whole calendar year for Vyvyan to recuperate from the operation. Vyvyan would be deaf in his left ear for the rest of his life – an irony, given that Vyvyan's ear problem was very similar to that of his father's final illness, and that his grandfather, Sir William Wilde, was an ear, nose and throat specialist doctor.

Vyvyan returned to Stonyhurst in January 1902 and would graduate from the Jesuit college in the summer of 1903 having passed the higher certificate examination, won another prize in Mathematics and the highly coveted *Praemium primi ordinis* – given to the boys who achieved ⅔ of the year's examination results.

During Vyvyan's final academic year at Stonyhurst, the family dismissed all the career options he suggested to them – including Jesuit brother and doctor. It was one thing to convert to a faith but to become clergy was not acceptable to a predominantly Protestant family. Becoming a doctor ran the risk of being associated with his paternal grandfather, Sir William Wilde. Initially, Vyvyan wanted to be a civil engineer, however this was not an option due to the deafness in his left ear. The family strongly felt a job in the Foreign Office based away from the UK would be his best option. Within a week of finishing at Stonyhurst, 17-year-old Vyvyan was dispatched to Switzerland the proud owner of a couple of new suits, a new bicycle, and a portmanteau and suitcase with his initials embossed upon them.

The summer months in the Swiss resort of Champery was spent playing lawn tennis, hiking and dancing. In September he went to help at a school in Lausanne, in what capacity or doing what Vyvyan is not specific in his autobiography. While there he was staying with an aunt who finally disclosed the truth of the scandal of his father.

His time in Switzerland came to an abrupt end after an unfortunate evening of excess drinking that found Vyvyan needing help home after drinking spirts for the first time. His Aunt wrote to the Napiers, who duly called him back, but not before sending him a puritan and over the top letter from his prim guardians, who clearly thought this one incident was proof that Vyvyan was heading down the same road as his father and would end up a debauched disgrace.

Poor Vyvyan. The Napiers' solution was to pack him off to Cambridge so that he could prepare for entry examinations. Cambridge had not been Vyvyan's preferred choice, he wanted to go to Oxford like his father – which, ironically, is the reason he was told he could not apply.

When Vyvyan arrived in Cambridge he lodged with a recent law graduate, Joshua Goodland, where he stayed to his room and studied for the entry exams. The hard work paid off as he not only passed, but passed very well and was accepted to study law the following academic year.

The rest of his summer was spent travelling with Goodland and two of his friends. Vyvyan had told his guardians that they were going to travel around Scandinavia, which had been true at the time. However, the party changed its mind at the last minute and decided to take a detour to Russia before heading to Sweden. In Russia Vyvyan visited Riga, St Petersburg, Moscow, Nizhny-Novgorod before returning to St Petersburg and finally going to Stockholm. The party remained in Sweden for the remainder of the summer before heading back so that Vyvyan could take his place at Trinity Hall, Cambridge – a college with a tradition of law students – for the year 1906/7. For the first time, Vyvyan Holland's life was vaguely normal.

It was around this time that Vyvyan started to become curious about his father's works and read some of them for the first time. He saw a copy of *The Ballad of Reading Gaol* on a friend's bookshelf and borrowed it. He had not even known of its existence until that point.

Finding copies of his father's work would prove rather difficult, even over a decade after his scandalous trial. Entries for Wilde in the university's library found the shelves empty apart from a single copy of *Intentions*. The best place to hunt for his father's works was in second-hand bookshops, but generally even then these were not original copies, but pirated copies often poorly printed. Cyril helped by sending his brother a copy of *De Profundis* for his nineteenth birthday.

Law did not grab Vyvyan as a subject but he found joy in editing the college magazine, *The Crescent*. At the end of the first academic year at Cambridge he decided not to complete his studies and pursue the career path chosen by his guardians. Before leaving Cambridge in the summer of 1907 Vyvyan confided his real identity to Joshua Goodland; his response was both kind and non-judgemental. He also told Vyvyan that Oscar was a great writer. Had these not been almost the same words the Jesuit priest had used when telling him of Oscar's death in Paris? His guardians attempt at keeping Oscar Wilde's connection to his sons was all for little to no purpose. Vyvyan soon realised that many people knew who his father was and had no problem with it.

He spent that summer mostly in Cambridge before returning to London, but not to the Napiers. Instead, he rented rooms in Kensington. He was staying in London in order to attend Scoones, an establishment that specialised in helping young men wanting to enter the Foreign Office. In order to do so candidates were required to sit and pass a Civil Service entry exam.

During this time Vyvyan needed to brush up on his forgotten and neglected German from his schooldays; his French, though good, was conversational rather than professional and needed amending, and he had a new subject to get an understanding of – Political Economy.

It was while he attended this Civil Service preparatory establishment, that Vyvyan would meet and become friends with Coleridge Arthur Fitzroy Kennard, who would go on to have a highly successful career as a diplomat. Kennard told Vyvyan that his mother, Mrs Hellen Carew, knew who he was and was eager to meet him as she had been a true and loyal friend of his father's. She had generously funded the purchase of Oscar's new burial plot in Paris's high-profile cemetery, Pere Lachaise.

Having read some of Oscar's works Vyvyan's curiosity had naturally been teased and he wanted to know more about his father, his work, and his parents' friends, so he was delighted to meet Coleridge's mother. And it was through Helen Carew that Vyvyan would meet his father's most loyal friend, Robert Ross.

At this first encounter, Vyvyan not only got to meet and start a great friendship with Ross, he would also met several other of Oscar's good friends too. Among that first gathering there was also Max Beerbohm and Reginald Turner, as well as Robbie Ross. Vyvyan's friendship with Ross would become lifelong until Ross died eleven years later in 1918.

Mrs Carew and Robbie would gradually introduce Oscar's youngest son to more of the people who had helped and cared for Oscar. One such person was Miss Adela Schuster, who had kindly paid for Wilde's defence in 1895. She also helped him financially after his release from Reading Gaol. It was also thanks to Miss Schuster, who had lovingly remembered and copied down fairy stories told by Oscar, that there are copies of them today. Vyvyan also met Mrs Ada Leverson who, with her husband, had sheltered Oscar when he was most in the spotlight and being pursued between his two trials in 1895.

Although Robbie Ross and Cyril had corresponded after Oscar's death, the two had never met. So it was arranged by Vyvyan that they would meet for dinner. The result was that Cyril made a new friend and he and Robbie would correspond frequently until Cyril's death in 1915. It would be Mrs Carew and Robbie Ross who organised Vyvyan's 21st Birthday celebrations. The party was held at Ross's home in Kensington, London, and the guests included American author Henry James, Reginald Turner, Coleridge Kennard, Ronald Fairbank, and his brother Cyril.

The following month Vyvyan went travelling with Joshua Goodland and one of their former travelling companions from the Russia trip, Peter Wallace. This time the friends headed west to Canada and they set sail on the RMS *Victorian* on 22 November 1907. In total they spent five months together in Canada before Vyvyan said goodbye to his friends, as they were heading towards Japan while he returned to Britain. Vyvyan travelled in his father's footsteps in that he caught a train from San Francisco to New York to return to England. On this journey home, Vyvyan had time to decide what to do for the future and he decided that the most sensible course of action was to complete his law exams for the bar.

He did not return to Cambridge straight away. He took rooms in Kensington and spent more time with Robbie Ross and Mrs Carew, who would introduce him to even more of his father's acquaintances, and great writers of the day including Thomas Hardy, H.G. Wells and Arnold Bennett.

One of Oscar's acquaintances that Vyvyan did not actively seek out, and only briefly engaged with over the years, was Alfred 'Bosie' Douglas. While at the theatre with Mrs Carew one evening Bosie happened to be behind them. Mrs Carew and Douglas exchanged pleasantries but did not introduce Vyvyan. The only other in-person meeting was at the coming out ball of Douglas's niece, Lady Jane Douglas, and the pair exchanged brief polite conversation and never saw each other again.

That is not to say that Vyvyan was not acquainted with the family. He would become friends with Bosie's nephew, Francis Archibald Kelhead Douglas, the 10th Marquess of Queensberry, who wrote a book entitled *Oscar Wilde and the Black Douglas*. It was published in 1949 and the marquess dedicated the book to Vyvyan.

In the summer of 1908 Vyvyan and Coleridge Kennard took a holiday in Venice, staying first on the lido then in the heart of the La Serenissima. Upon their return the friends met up with Kennard's mother in Paris, and she showed Vyvyan where his father had died. They returned in time for September when started again at Cambridge to achieve his bar exams, completing his studies in the summer of 1909. In the summer of 1909, Robbie Ross and Vyvyan travelled to Paris to oversee the relocation of Oscar's remains from Bagneux Cemetery to Pere Lachaise.

Having completed his law studies Vyvyan would be called to the bar in 1912 as part of Inner Temple's Inn of Court. Two years after this he married his first wife, Violet Mary Craigie, but the marriage would end in tragedy as Violet died from injuries sustained in a fire on 15 October 1918.

Vyvyan, like his brother Cyril, did his part in the First World War. He served as a Second Lieutenant in the Interpreters Corps, before later joining the Royal Field Artillery. He was lucky to survive the horrors of the western front, unlike his brother and many other men of his generation. He would be demobilised from the army on 27 July 1919, and would be awarded an OBE for his actions during the war.

After being widowed in 1918, Vyvyan remained unmarried for twenty-five years before marrying his second wife, Dorothy Thelma Helen Besant. The pair married in September 1943 and had their only child, Christopher Merlin Vyvyan Holland, in December 1945.

During the Second World War Vyvyan worked for the BBC as a translator and editor rather than returning to the trenches to fight. After the war he and his new family decided to relocate to Dorothy's homeland, Australia, where they lived in Melbourne from 1948 until 1952. By this time Vyvyan had followed in his father's footsteps and had gained a reputation as a writer in his own right. After 1952 the family returned to London, where Vyvyan lived the rest of his life, dying at the age on 80 on the 10 October 1967.

In many ways Vyvyan was his parents', but particularly Oscar's, greatest legacy. He not only survived a tragic start in life, but he went on to thrive personally, privately and professionally. Many of the choices he made were ones Oscar considered, such as converting to Catholicism, and they had been done without knowledge of his father's thoughts on these matters. It is also through many of his works that we have access to insightful and poignant aspects of Oscar Wilde the man, rather than the Oscar Wilde portrayed by the press and by history books.

When Oscar Wilde died on 30 November 1900, he had appointed his most loyal friend Robert Ross as his literary executor. When he died in Paris, Oscar Wilde had very little to his name and had accumulated debts including to the hotel was his last home and where he breathed his last.

After the scandal of his trials and subsequent conviction and imprisonment, many of Oscar's works became hard to find, as his youngest son Vyvyan found out, while at Cambridge University. This, of course, meant that the estate could not generate income from his existing published catalogue. This was further complicated by the fact that Wilde's estate was not the copyright holder to all his work. One of the things Robbie Ross would do was buy back these copyrights for the estate.

It was not all bad news, however. Although his written published works were hard to find, performances of his plays did continue even at the end of his life. Often, though, Wilde's name was not advertised and the plays were performed on touring theatrical circuits as well as widely performed within Europe; particularly in France and Germany.

The most successful and profitable of these works was one of his most controversial plays – *Salomé*. It remained banned in the United Kingdom until 1907 due to its perceived blasphemous content. This did not put off European audiences and it was frequently and widely performed in both France and Germany.

Another way to make the Wilde estate solvent again was to publish a highly edited version of Wilde's letter to Bosie written in Reading Gaol, as *De Profundis*. This edited version was an elegantly written and insightful meditation on the ideas and theories of punishment and repentance. The work proved to be popular and went a long way in restoring public opinion of Oscar Wilde. It is just a shame that it happened posthumously rather than in those sad broken last years in exile.

In the mid- to late twentieth century, Wilde became en vogue once again, both for his literary and dramatical works but also as a positive LGBT+ hero and icon, becoming important during a time in history when the gay community were fighting for equal legal rights in the UK.

Many of his works have also been reinstated into exam curriculums, in particular *The Picture of Dorian Gray* is studied by many GCSE student in the UK, examining the language and various themes Wilde explores in his only novel. These works are not just studied by English speaking students either.

Although Oscar Fingal O'Flahertie Wills Wilde never actually declared his genius to US customs, it is fair to say that thanks to the hard work and dedication of his loyal friend Robbie Ross, his legacy of work declares that genius over a century after many of his works were first published, as well as remaining relevant to modern audiences. His works, as well as the success of his son Vyvyan, are his greatest legacies.

CONCLUSIONS

Through the research for this book, and evidence presented, I hope I have been able to present the *real* Oscar Wilde. It is very easy to form perceptions, opinions and stereotypes of historical figures based upon how they were projected to the world, or through their different works or their reputations, be it good, bad or scandalous. In the case of Oscar Wilde, he presented all these perspectives to his contemporaries, as well as to his future audiences and we, the reader or the historian, have formed a stereotypical image and concept of who Mr Oscar Wilde was and how he lived.

Through looking at lesser-known aspects of Oscar Wilde's life, such as his childhood and parents, his education, the subjects he studied and at which he excelled, we get an idea how his personality was formed. We can understand even more through his choice of wife, and how she differed from the average Victorian woman. By looking at the lesser known pieces of his work, the lectures from his American tour and his prominent role within the Aesthetic Moment, we can better comprehend his works and how he presented himself to the world. By examining his relationship with his sons, along with their recollections of their father, we have a greater understanding of the family man, rather than simply the wit and personality many think of upon hearing the name Oscar Wilde. Lastly, by exploring Wilde at his most vulnerable, on trial, in prison, and struggling to cope after prison, I hope I have been able to present a fuller, more well-rounded, *real* image of Oscar Fingal O'Flahertie Wills Wilde; the son, the brother, the student, the private man, the public persona, the aesthete, the husband, the father, the prisoner, the exile, the lover, the friend.

He was a man of great feelings and emotions, he was able to self-reflect and see his faults, but he was also fallible in that he, like many of us, choose to pursue and re-establish happiness where he had found pain, disappointment and betrayal. He was guilty of being proud, stubborn, flippant, angry, he held grudges and was at times selfish – in short, he was human. Many of these less attractive qualities were exaggerated while he was in the company of Bosie.

Equally, he was a loyal friend, generous to the point of being too generous, empathetic and always willing to help when he felt something was wrong, even if it was detrimental financially or to his reputation. He was a man of strong politics, favouring fairer socialist ideals – although this was more theoretical idealism than lived experience. Due to his social status and profession and his taste for luxury, Oscar Wilde could have never lived as socialist. Although he never returned to live in his native Ireland after he graduated from Oxford university, his Irish nationalist sympathies were also reflective of his pride in being an Irishman.

With hindsight, the tragedy is knowing that had Wilde not met Lord Alfred Douglas, Bosie, in 1891, he may have lived longer, written more plays, or even more novels, as well as having a less tragic ending. But the path he took did mean that, in my opinion, he produced two of his best pieces of work, the haunting and beautifully worded *Ballad of Reading Gaol* and the self-reflective and extraordinary work that was published as *De Profundis* after his death.

In today's enlightened, more empathetic, tolerant and secular society, the majority of us would be outraged if a person was harassed as Wilde was by the Marquess of Queenserry. Then subsequently arrested and imprisoned for two years' hard labour for consensual sexual relations between two persons of the same gender. Many others in Wilde's situation were able to go into exile rather than face trial and then the inevitable imprisonment. Oscar however saw this as cowardly, he wanted to face the charges. This brave, principled and conscientious decision says much about Wilde's character and disposition. Sadly, there are still people around the world who live in fear of persecution for loving some one of their own sex, I hope that the history and story of Oscar Wilde gives them hope that one day they too will live in an enlightened and tolerant society.

Oscar Wilde the playwright, poet and novelist, left an amazing legacy. Very few people in history are quoted as frequently in everyday speech, but Mr Wilde is one of those who is; therefore, even though he never actually said that he had nothing to declare but his genius, he did in fact leave a legacy of work declaring it for him. One of the reasons Oscar Wilde is so readily quoted, read, watched, performed and still fascinates people, nearly 125 years after his death, is because his works are still relatable and relevant, even today. His works are a projection of his open minded, liberal outlook, and reflect that he was not afraid to be an individual, in a time when conformity was the social norm.

BIBLIOGRAPHY

Brandon, Ruth, *Being Divine: a Biography of Sarah Bernhardt*, Mandarin Paperbacks, 1992

Edmonds, Antony, *Oscar Wilde's Scandalous Summer – The 1894 Worthing Holiday and the aftermath*, Amberley Publishing, 2014

Fitzsimons Eleanor, *Wilde's Women, How Oscar Wilde Was Shaped By The Women He Knew* Duckworth Overlook, 2015

Frankel, Nicholas, *Oscar Wilde the Unrepentant Years*, Harvard University Press, 2017

Gray, Frances, *York Notes on The Picture of Dorian Gray*, Longman, 2001

Hanberry, Gerard, *More Lives Than One. The remarkable Wilde Family Through The Generations*, Colins Press, 2011.

Harris Frank, *Oscar Wilde His life & Confessions*, Create Space Independent Publishing, 2015

Holland, Merlin & Hart Davis, Rupert (eds) *The complete letters of Oscar Wilde,* Fourth Estate Publishing, 2000

Holland, Merlin, *Irish Peacock & Scarlet Marquess – The Real Trial of Oscar Wilde*, Fourth Estate, 2003 (A transcript of the libel case against the Marquess of Queensberry)

Holland, Vyvyan, *Son of Oscar Wilde*, Carroll & Graf Publishers INC, revised edition 1999

Montgomery Hyde, *Oscar Wilde: A Biography*, Penguin, 2001

Montgomery Hyde, *Oscar Wilde: The Aftermath*, Methuen, 1963

Moyle, Franny, *Constance, The Tragic and Scandalous Life of Mrs Oscar Wilde*, Hachette, 2011

Murray, Douglas, *Bosie, The tragic Life of Lord Alfred Douglas*, Holder & Stouhton, 2000

Nassaar Christopher S, *York Notes on The Importance of Being Earnest*, Longman, York Press, 1987

Sturgis Matthew, *Oscar a Life*, Head of Zeus, 2019

Wilde, Oscar, *Complete Poetry*, Oxford University Press, 2009

Wilde, Oscar, *Only Dull People Are Brilliant At Breakfast*, Penguin Classics, 2016

Wilde Oscar, Ed. Frankel Nicholas, *The annotated Prison Writings of Oscar Wilde*, Harvard University Press, 2018

Wilde Oscar, *The Picture of Dorian Gray*, Ward, Lock and Company, London, 1891

Wilde Oscar, *The Importance of Being Earnest*, Chiswick Press, London, 1898

Wilde Oscar, *An Ideal Husband*, Chiswick Press, London, 1898

Wilde Oscar, *Salomé*, Libraire de L'art Indépendant, Paris, 1893

Periodicals & Journals

The Lancet, 3 January 2015, Volume 385, Issue 9962 'The Enigmatic illness and death of Constance, Wife of Oscar Wilde'

Hearth & Home in June 1896

Websites

OscarWildeinamerica.org – a brilliant resource that has details of all his lectures given in 1882 in the US.

INDEX